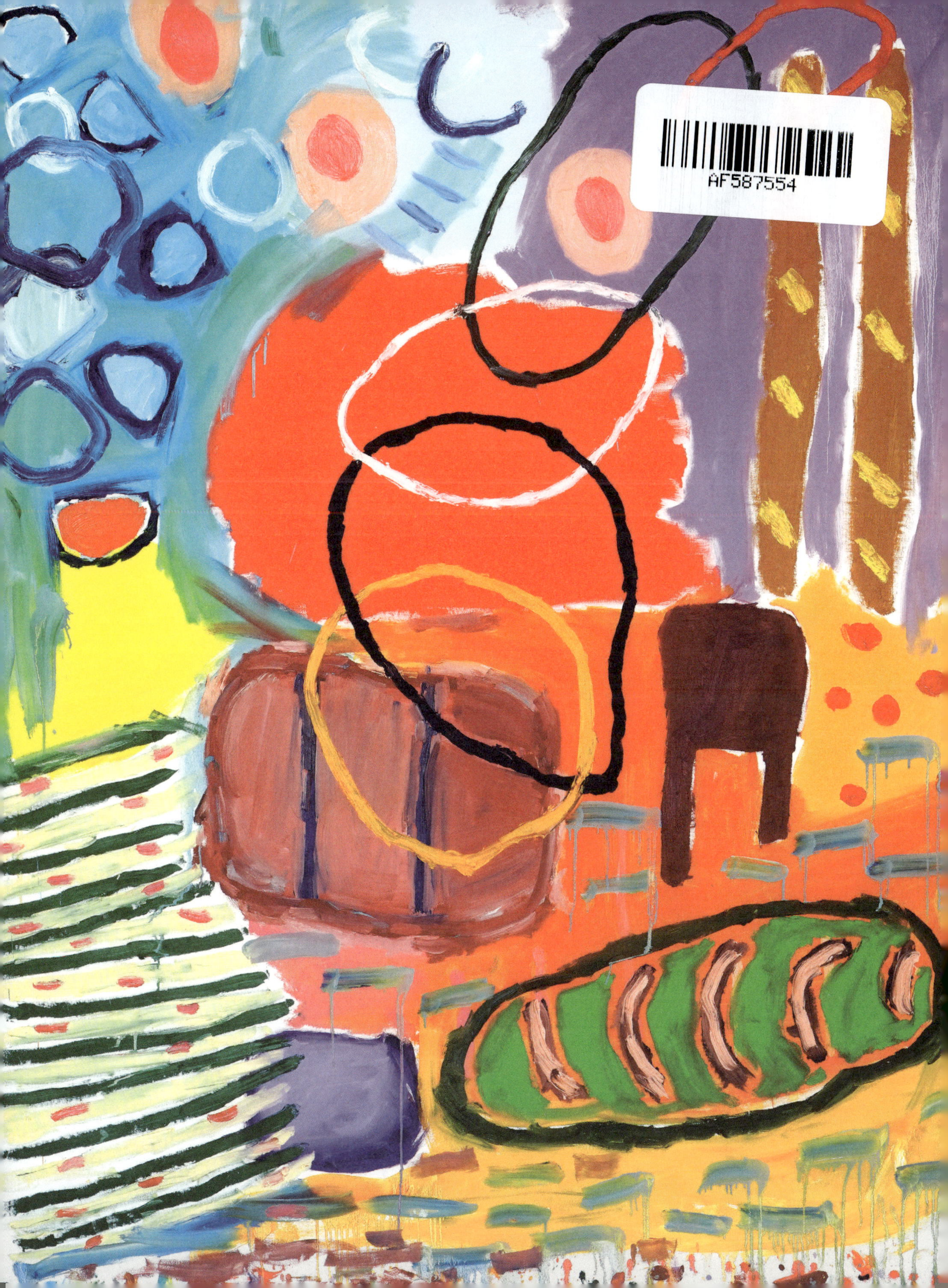

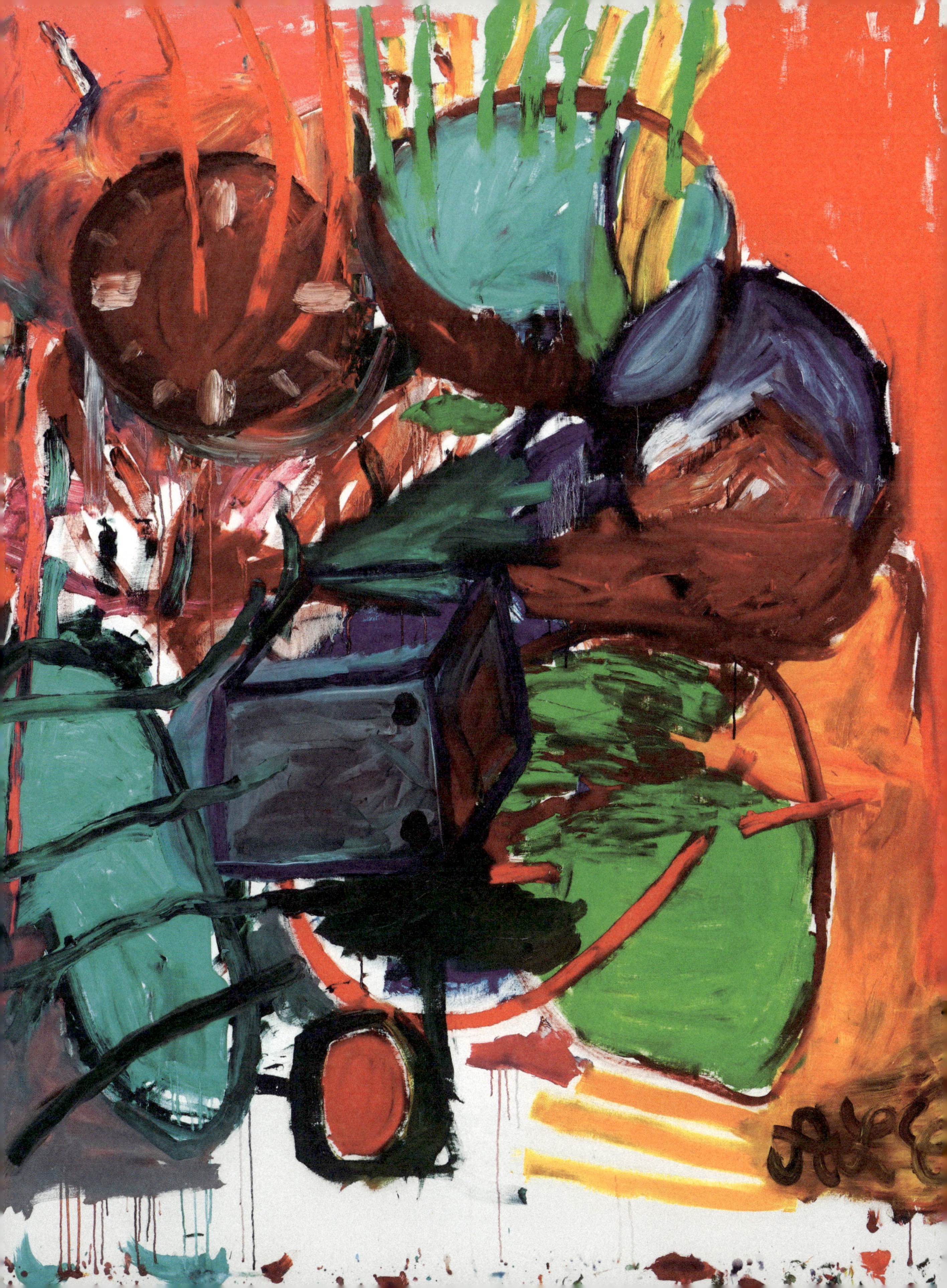

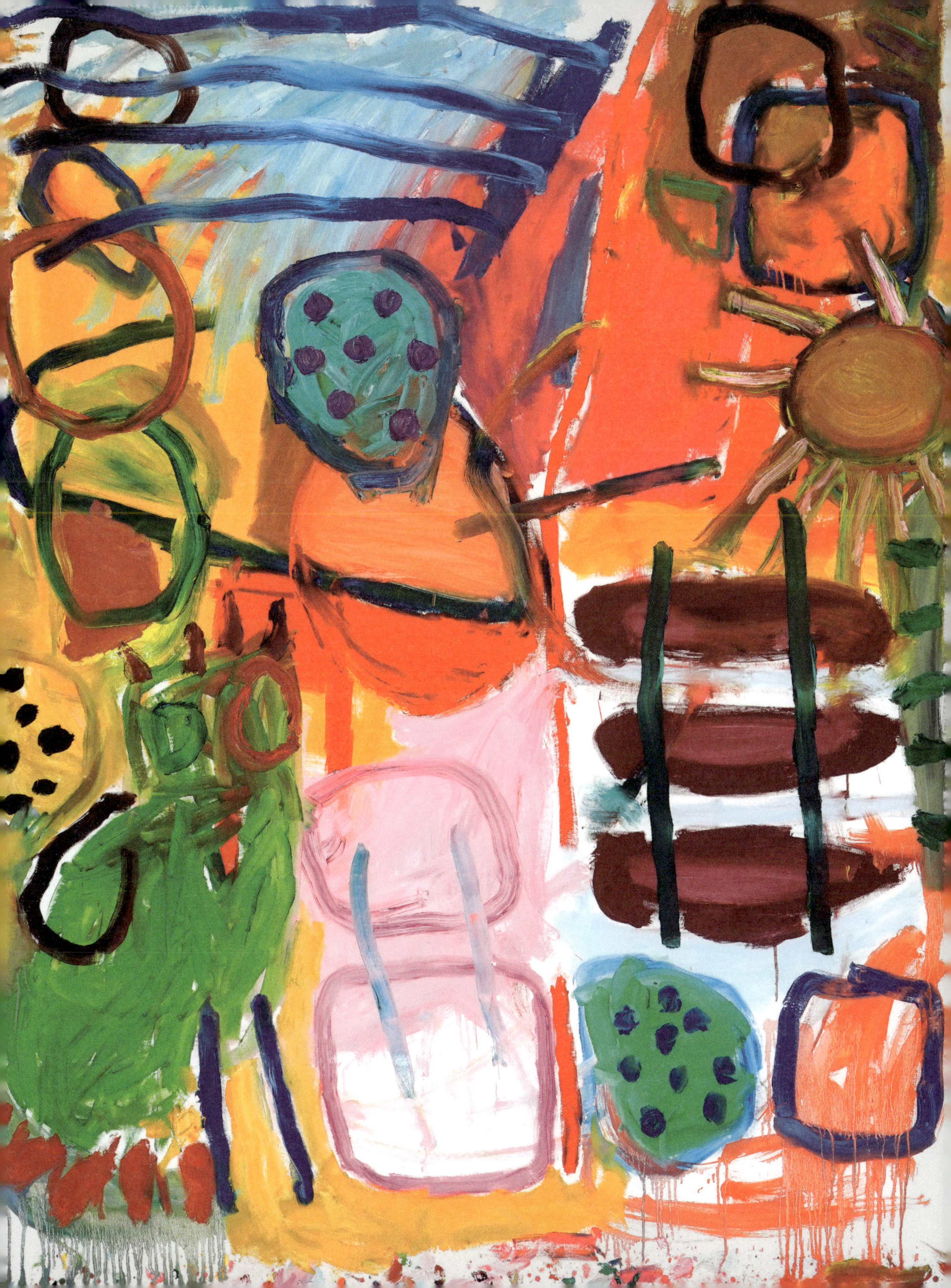

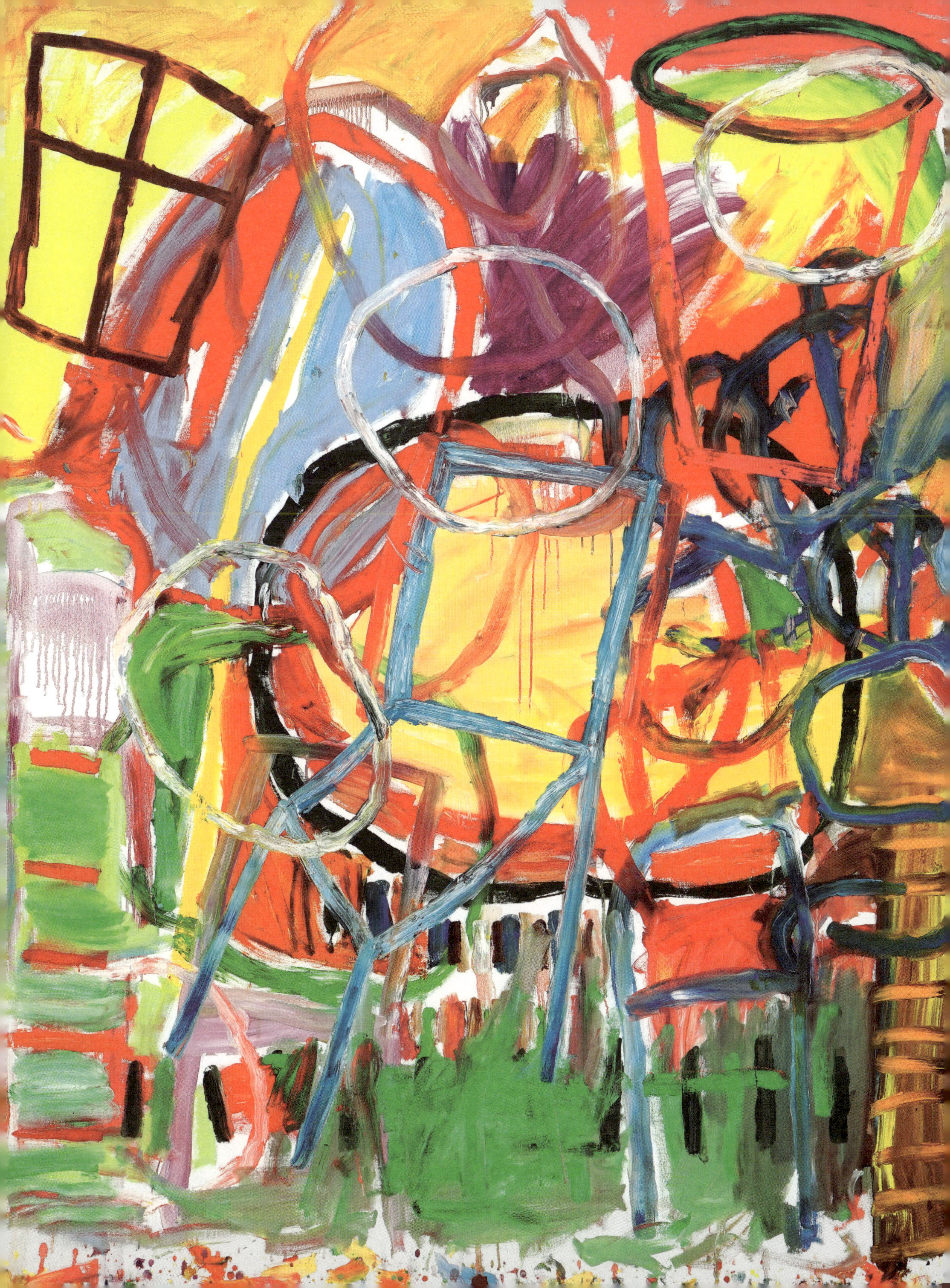

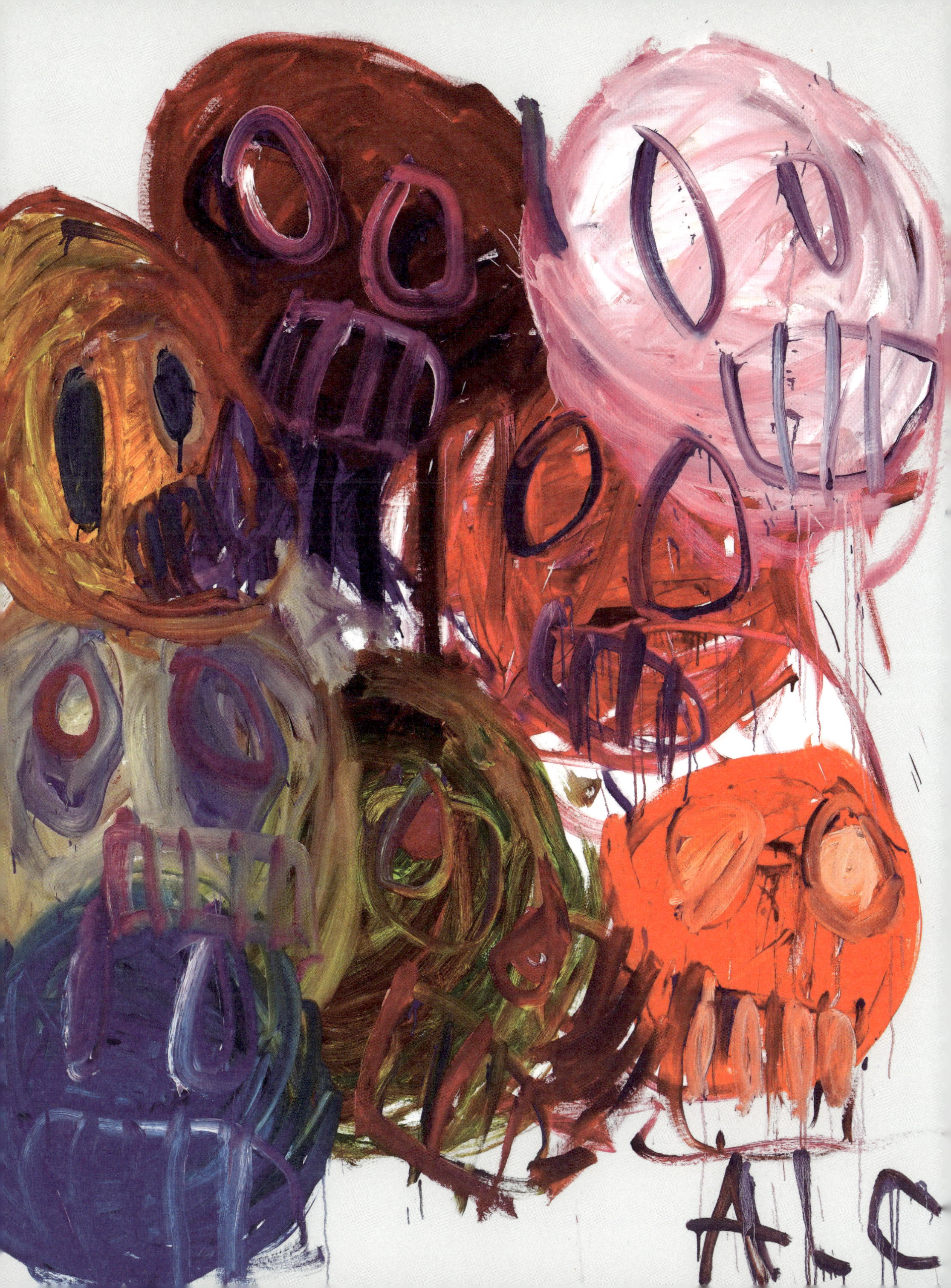
ALC

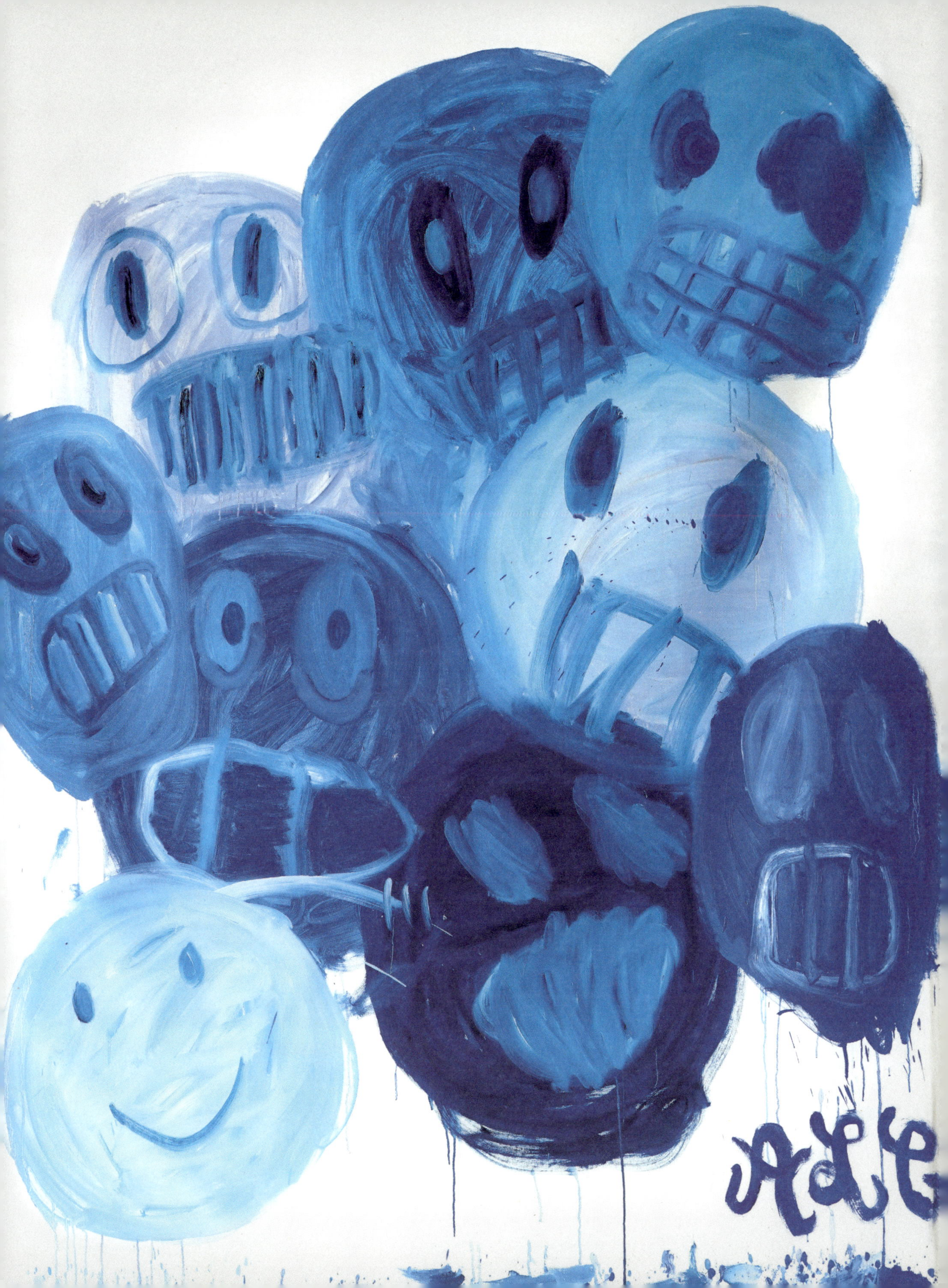

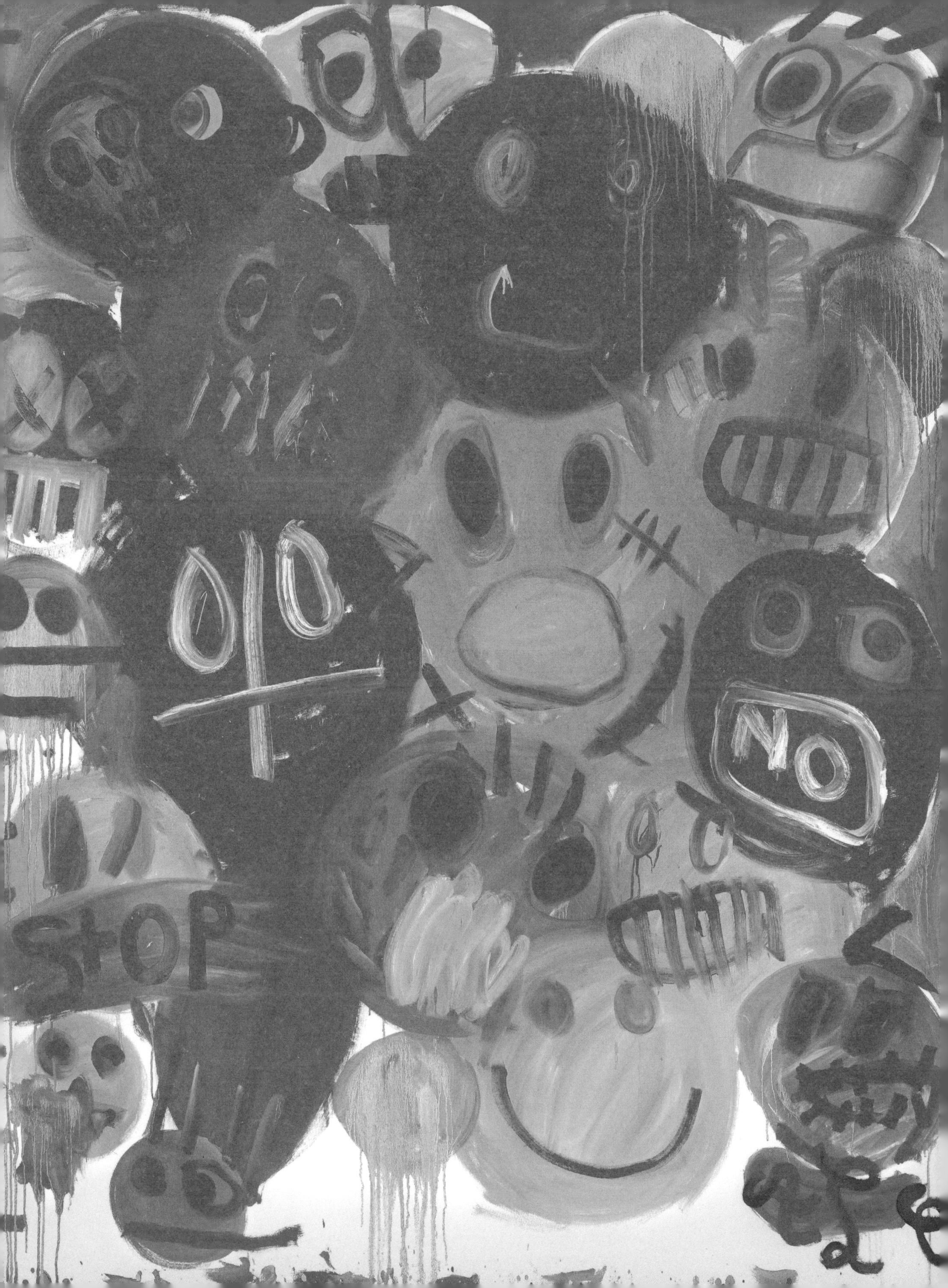
NO
STOP

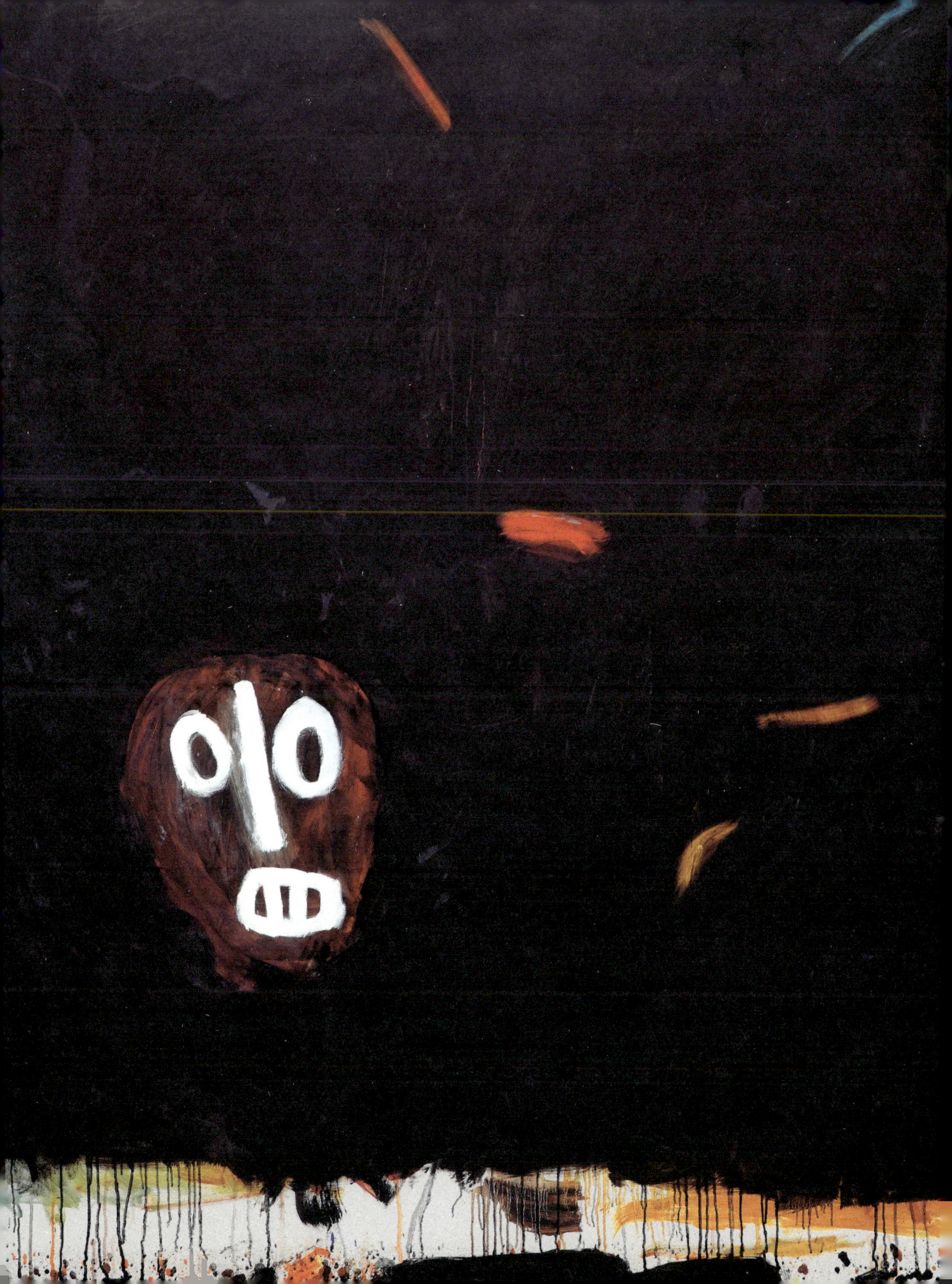

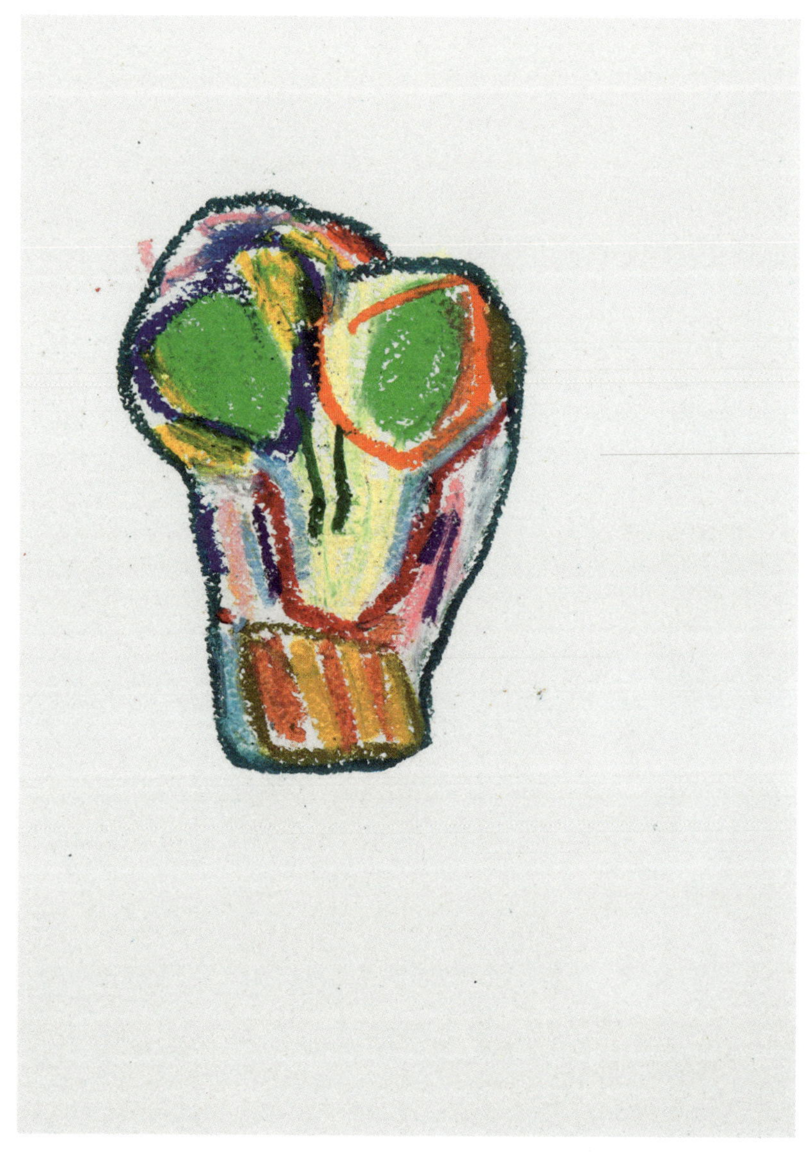

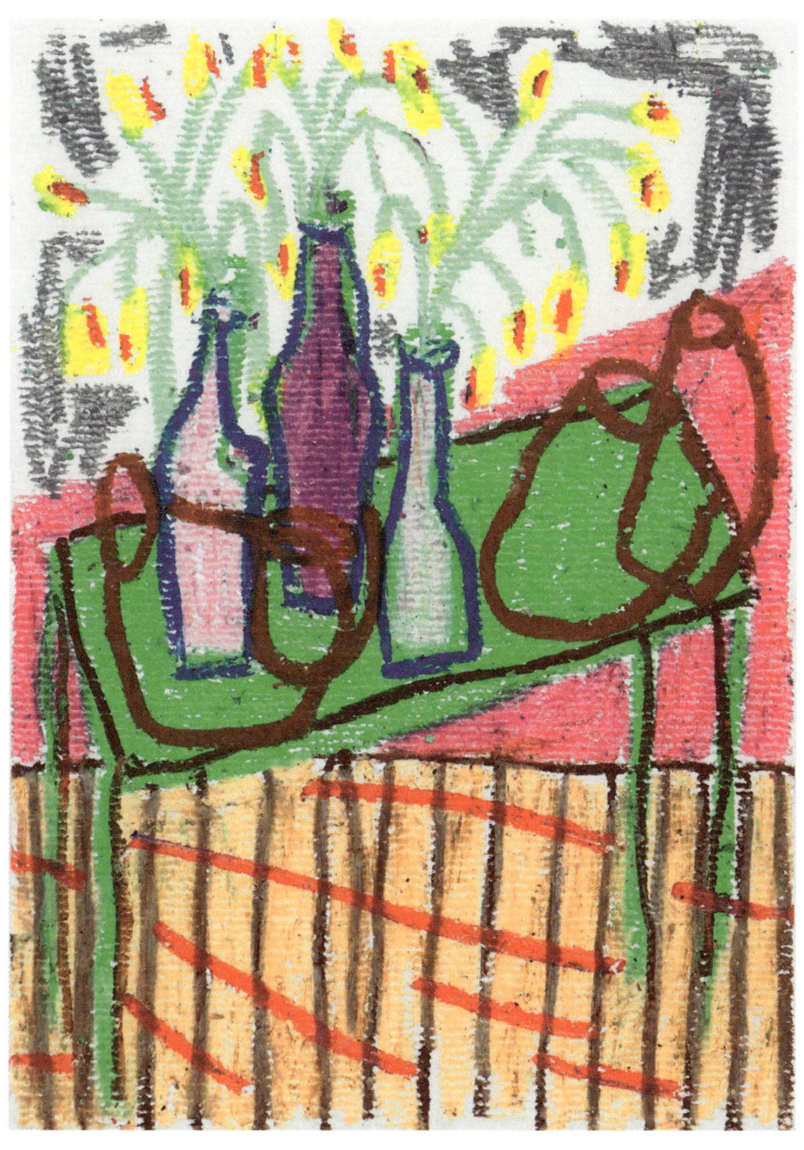

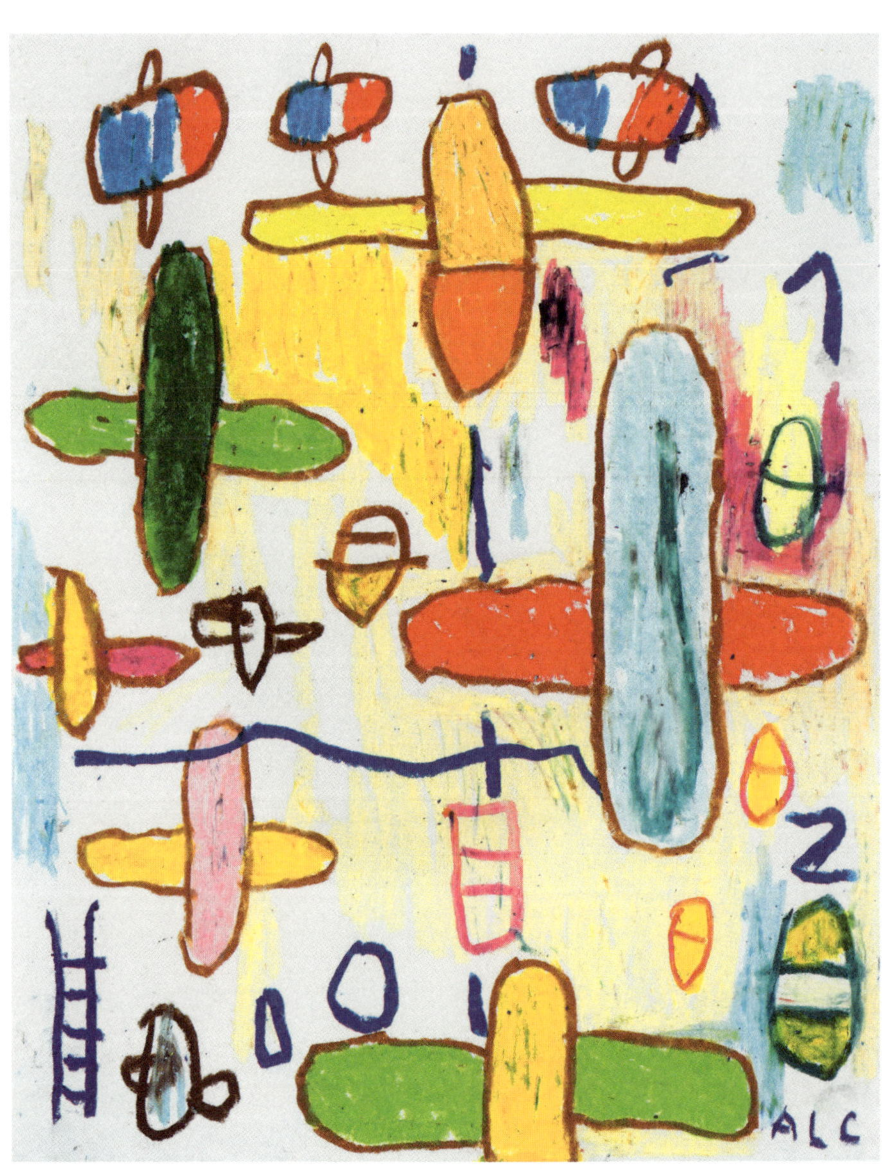
ALC

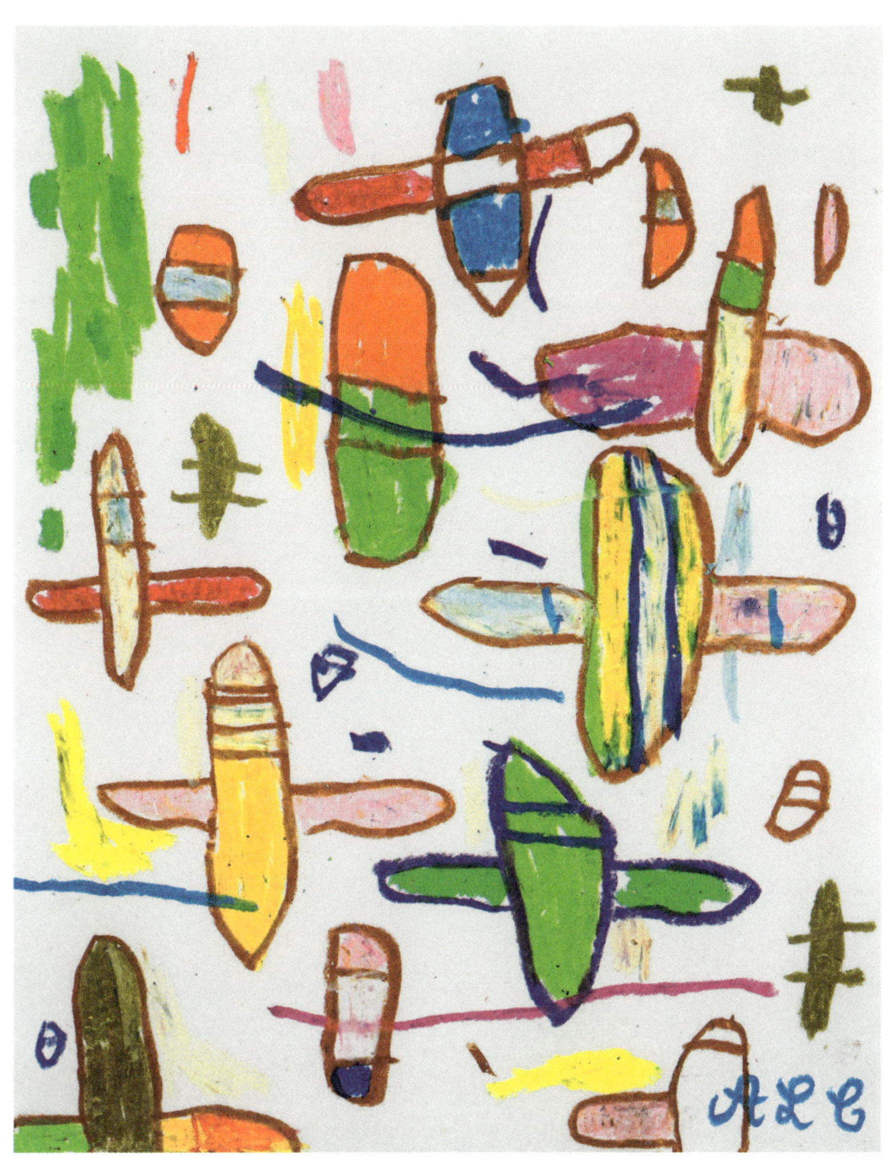
ALC

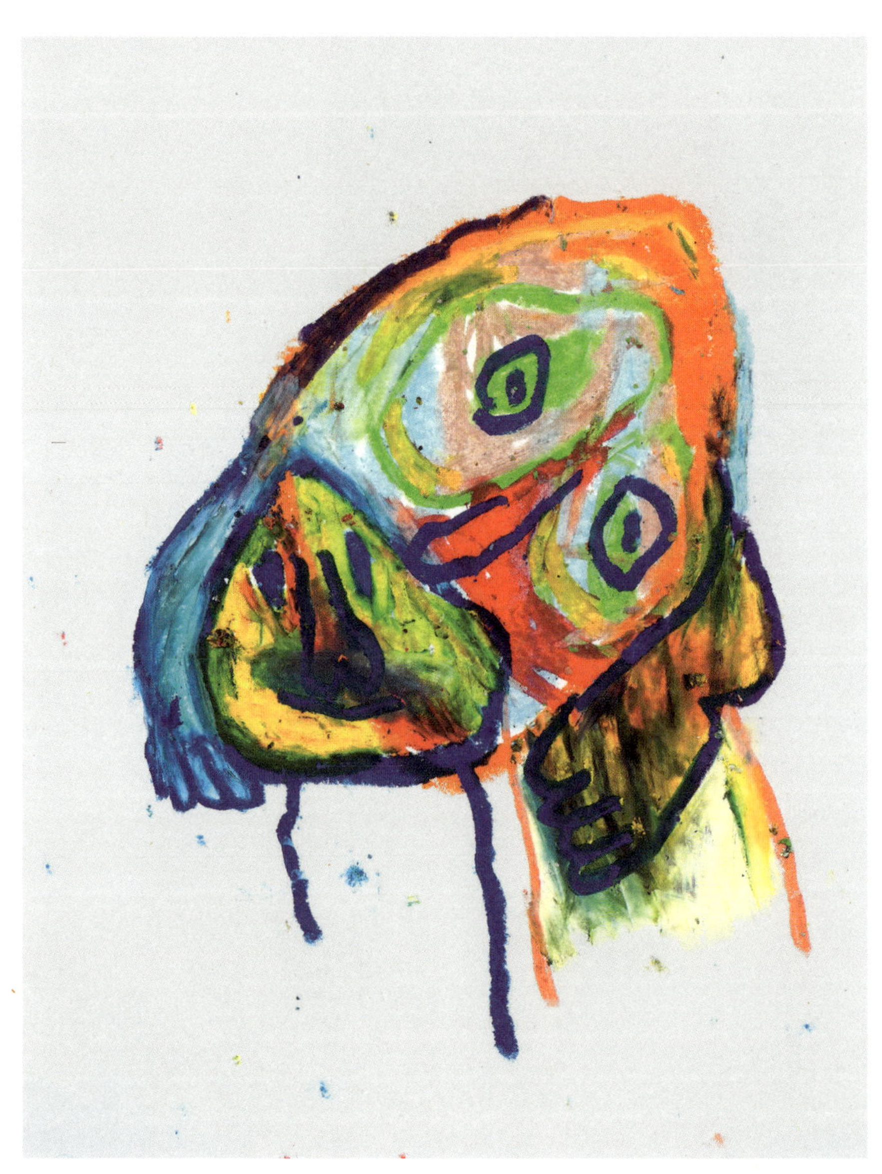

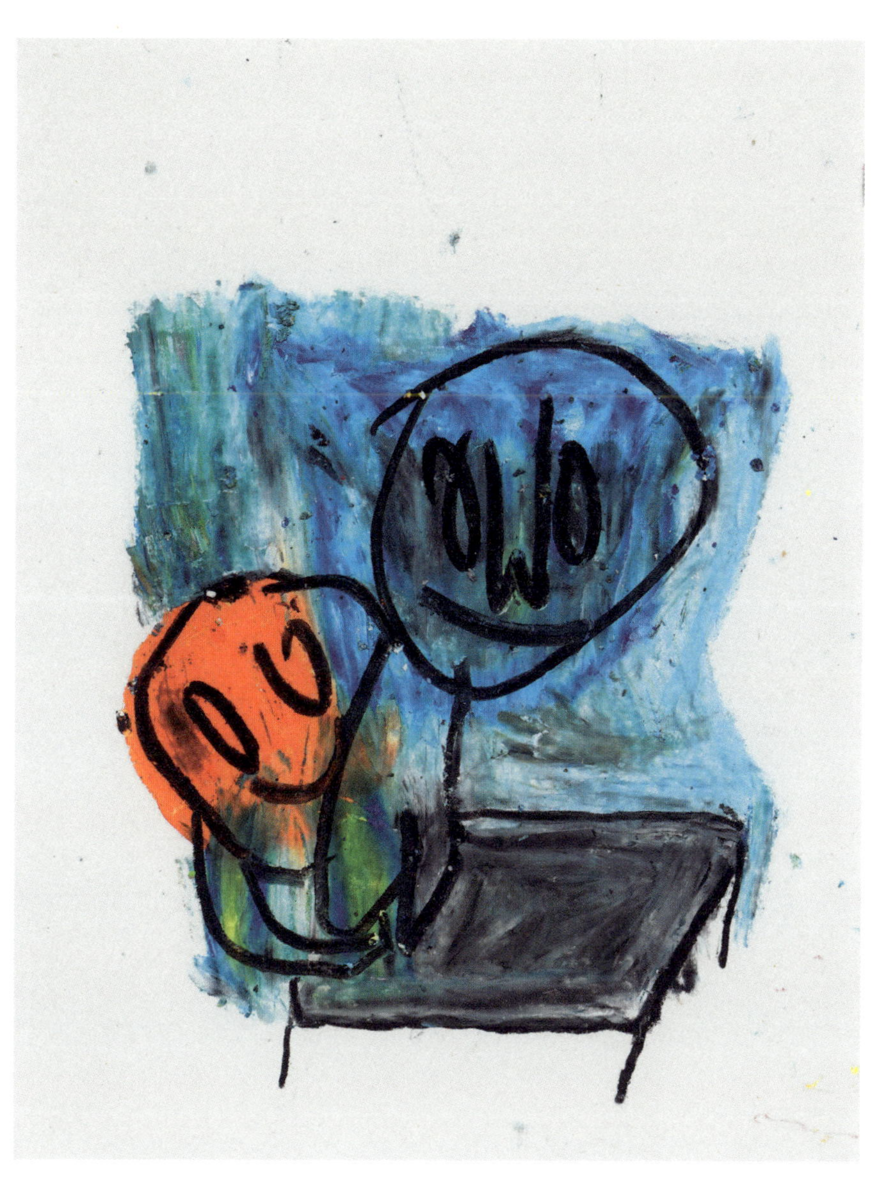

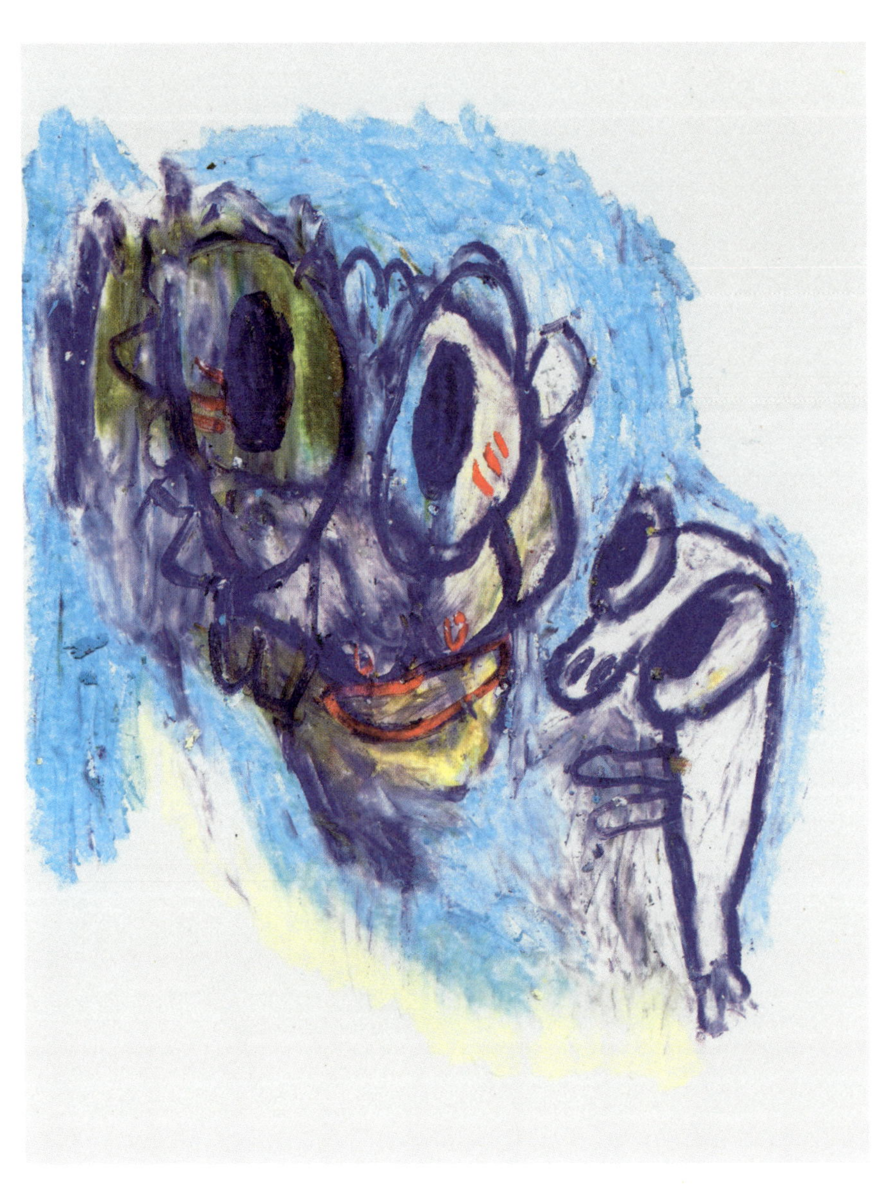

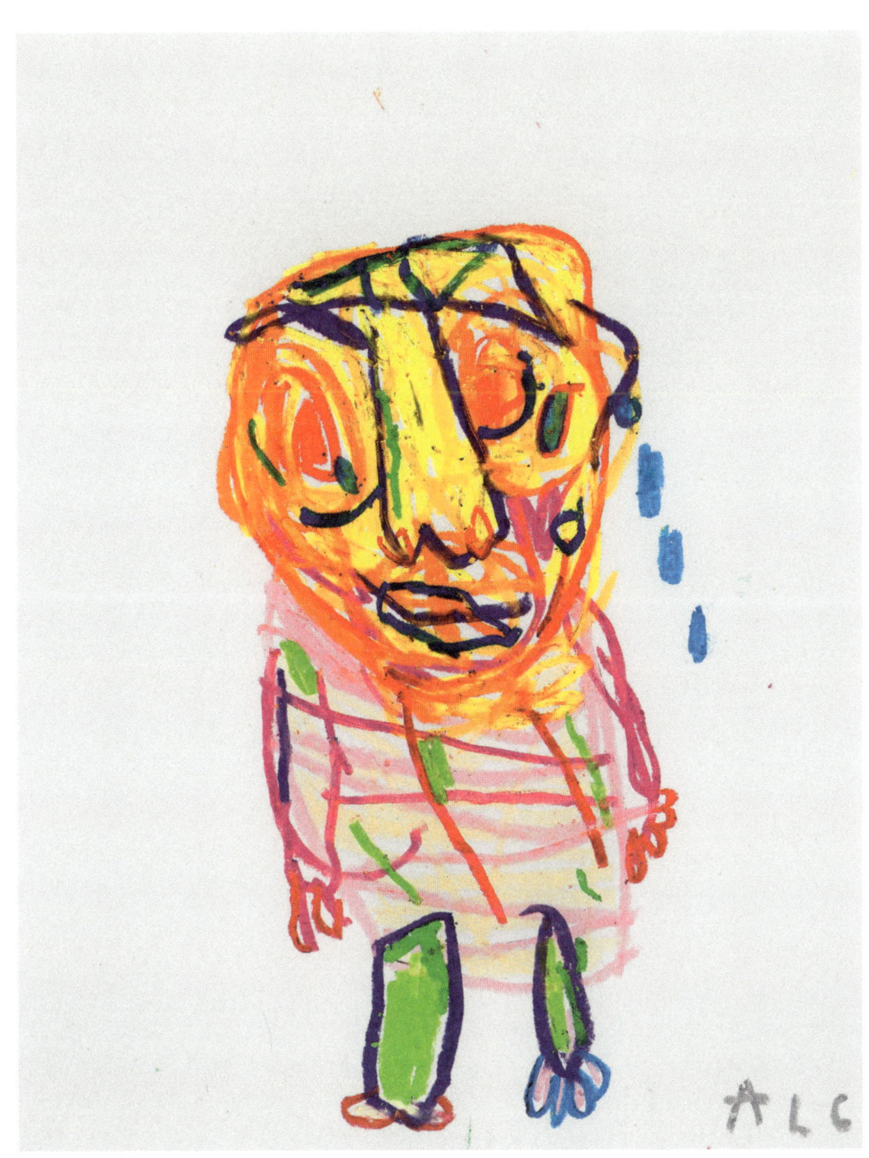
ALC

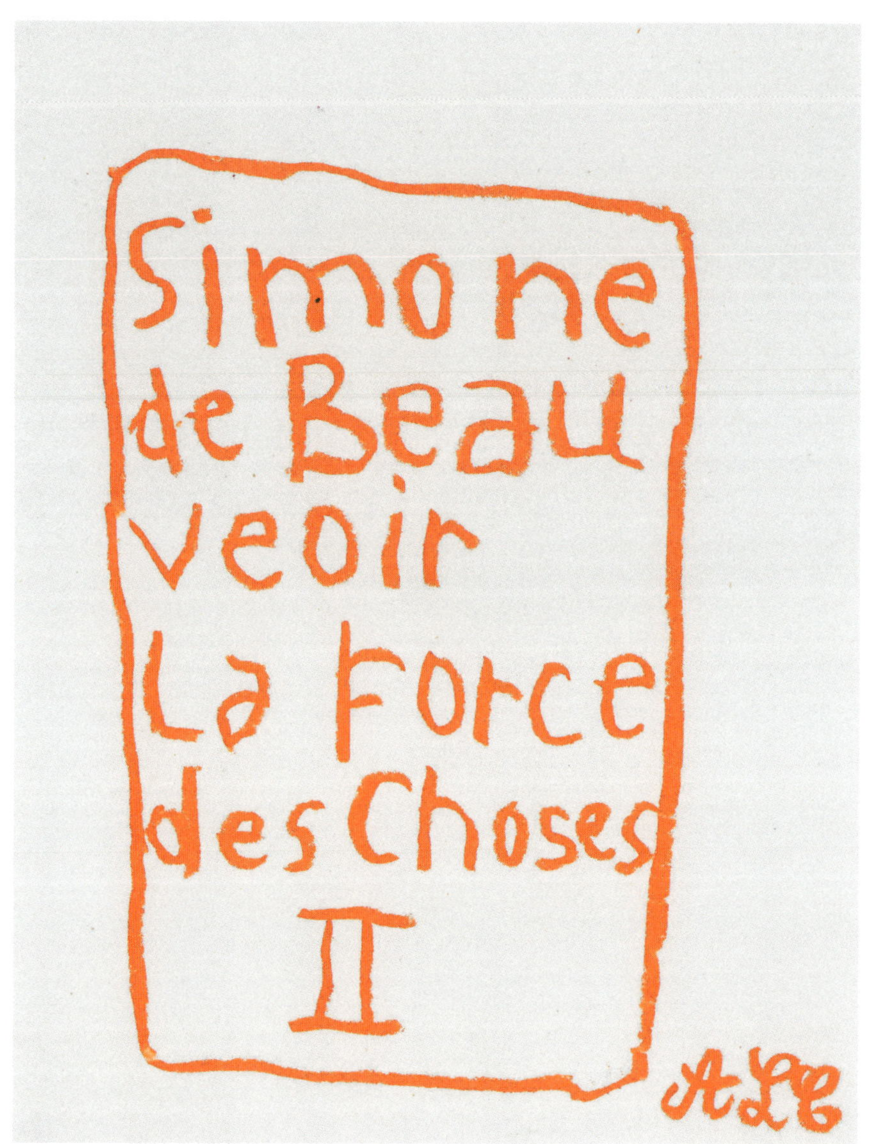
Simone
de Beau
veoir
La Force
des Choses
II
ALC

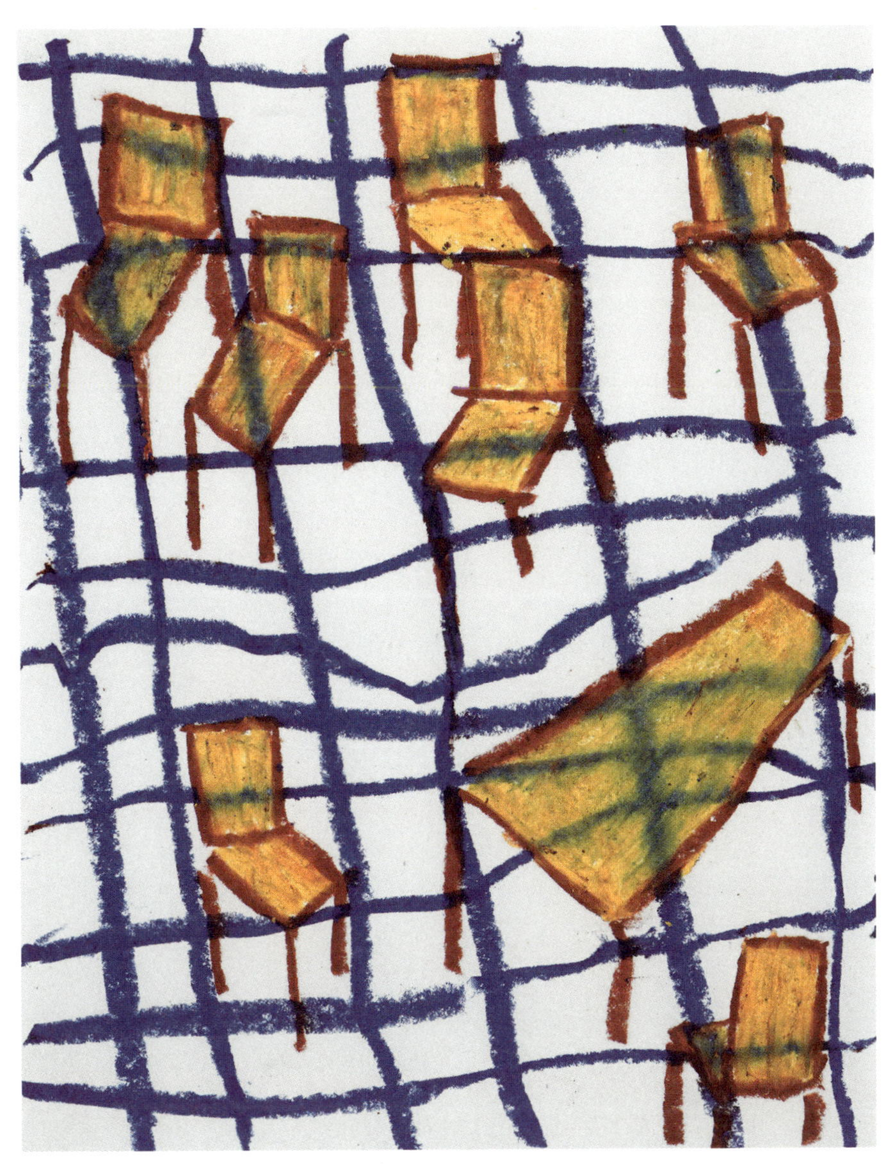

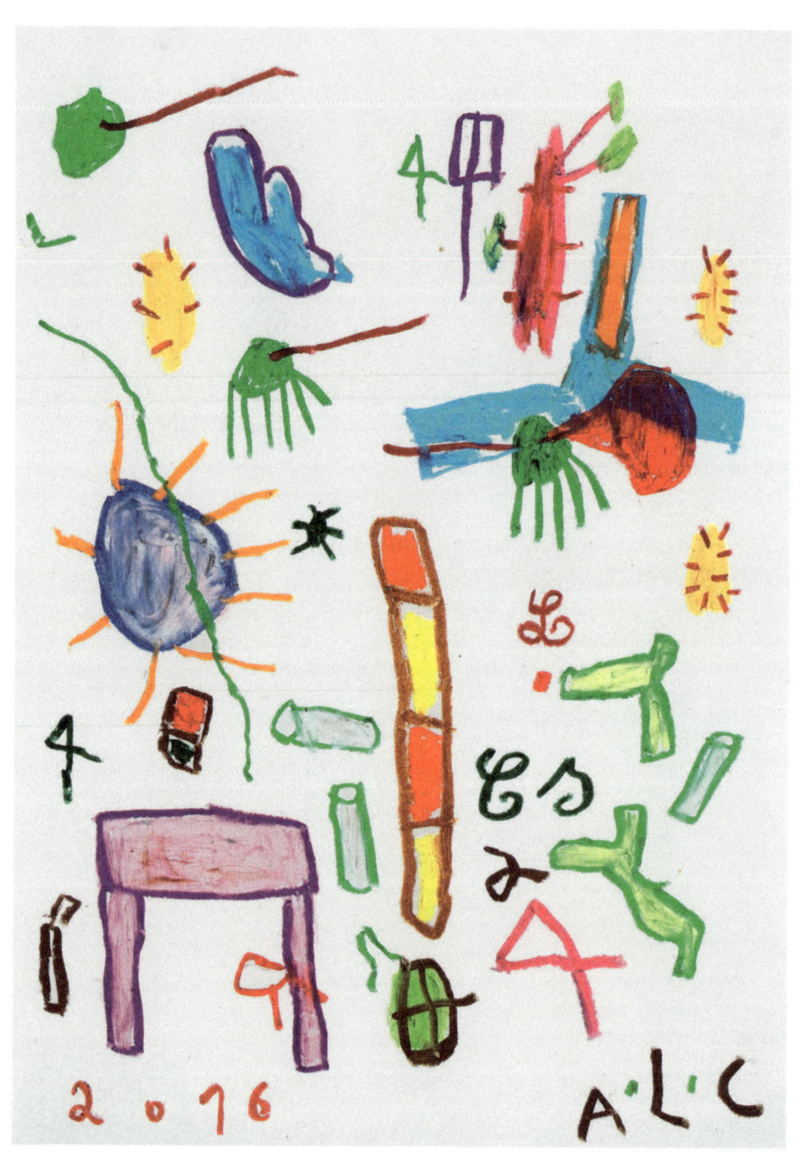
2016
A L C

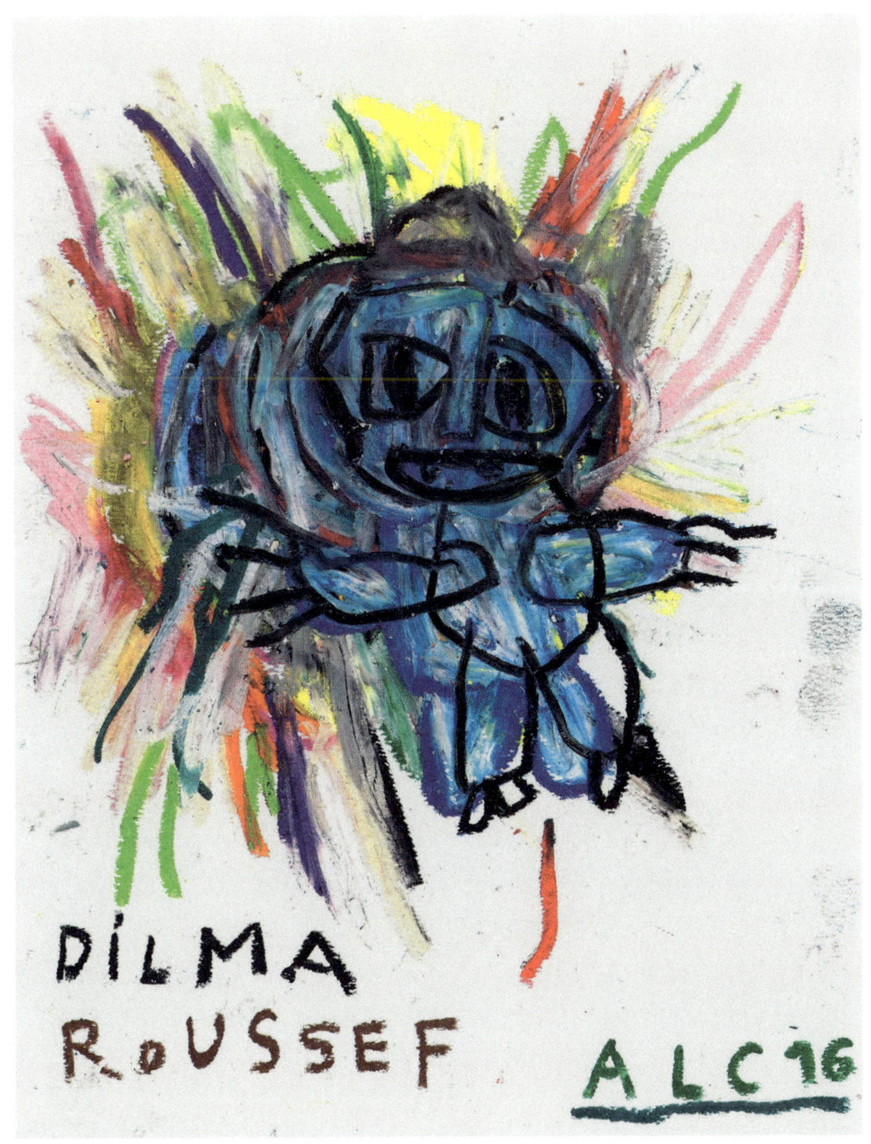
DiLMA
RoUSSEF
ALC16

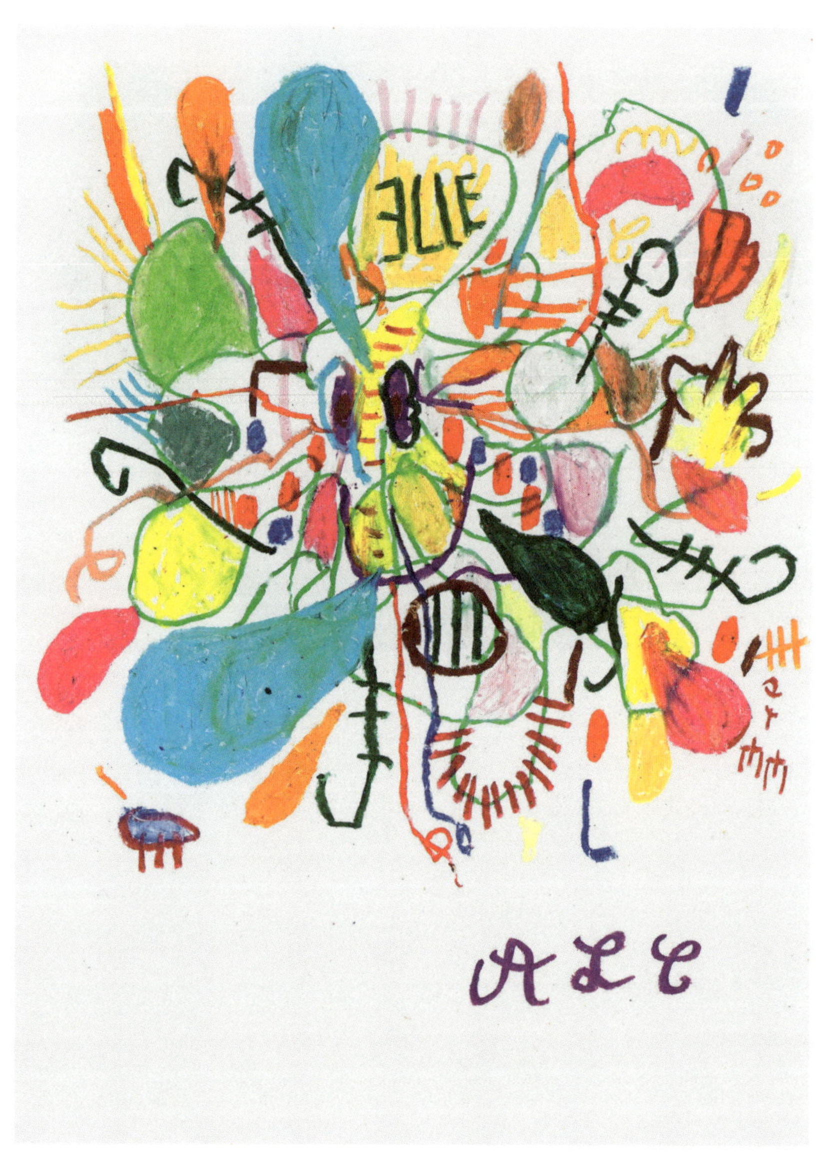
ALC

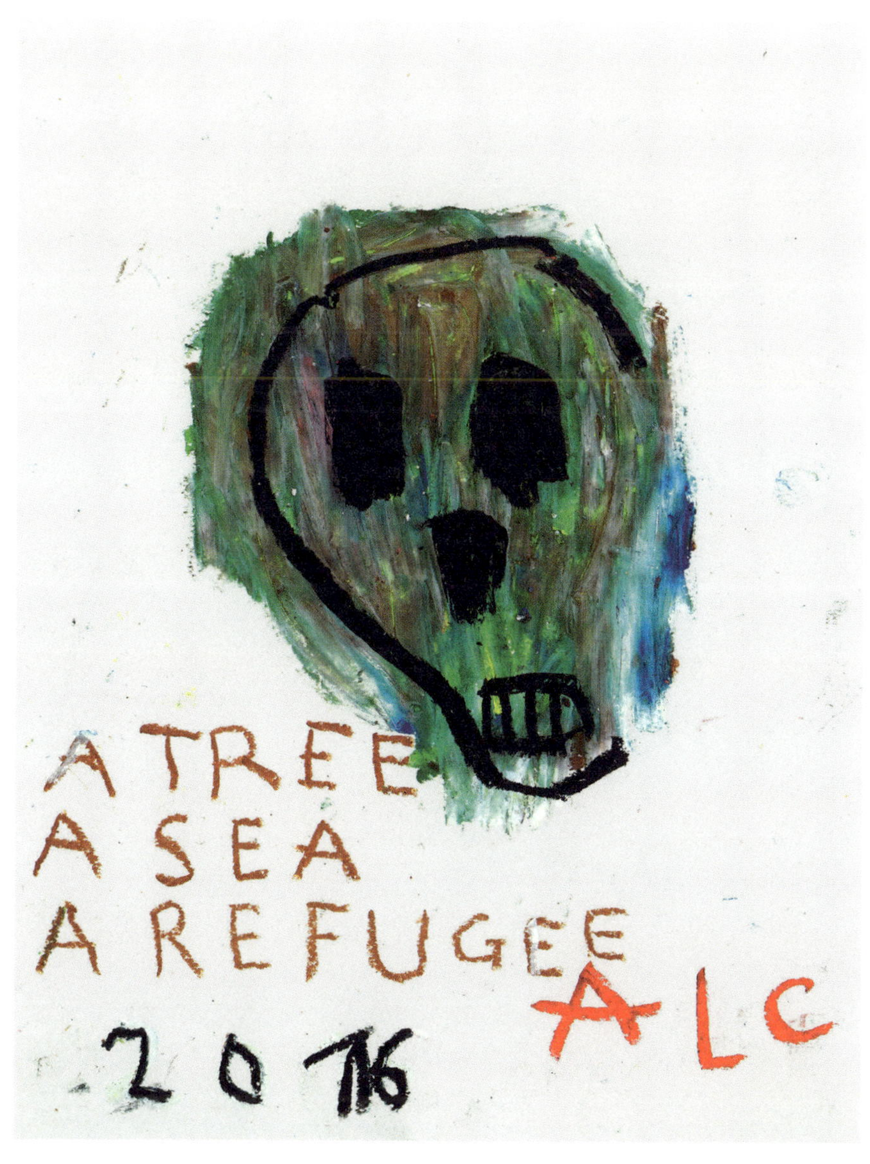
A TREE
A SEA
A REFUGEE
ALC
2016

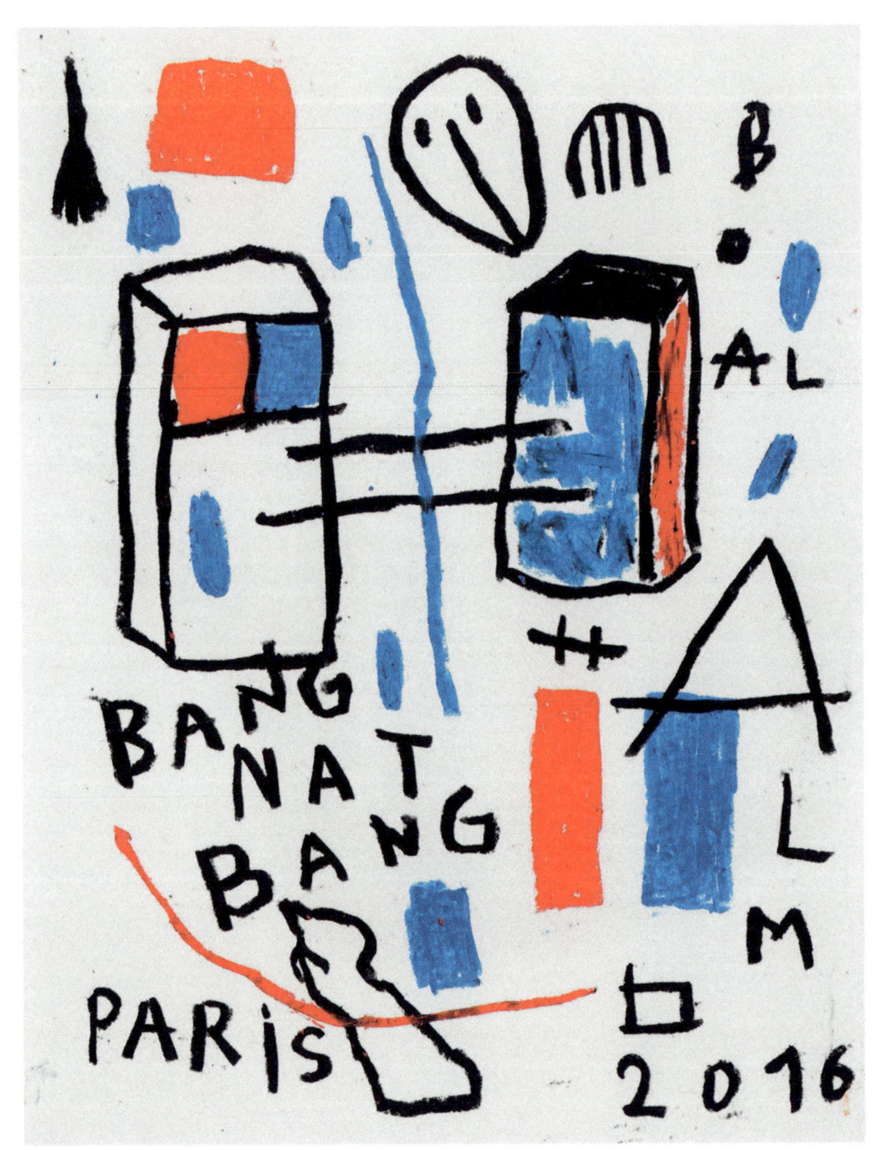
AL
BANG
NAT
BANG
L
M
PARIS
2016

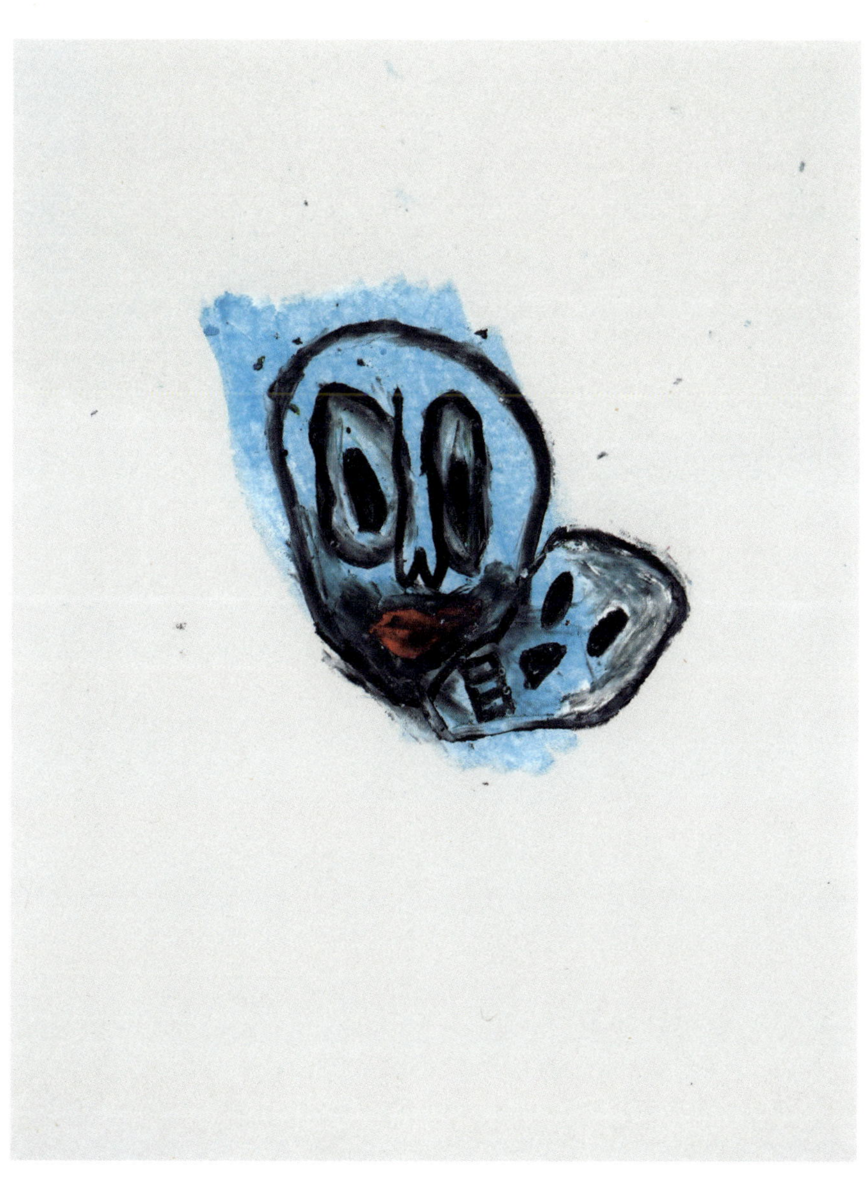

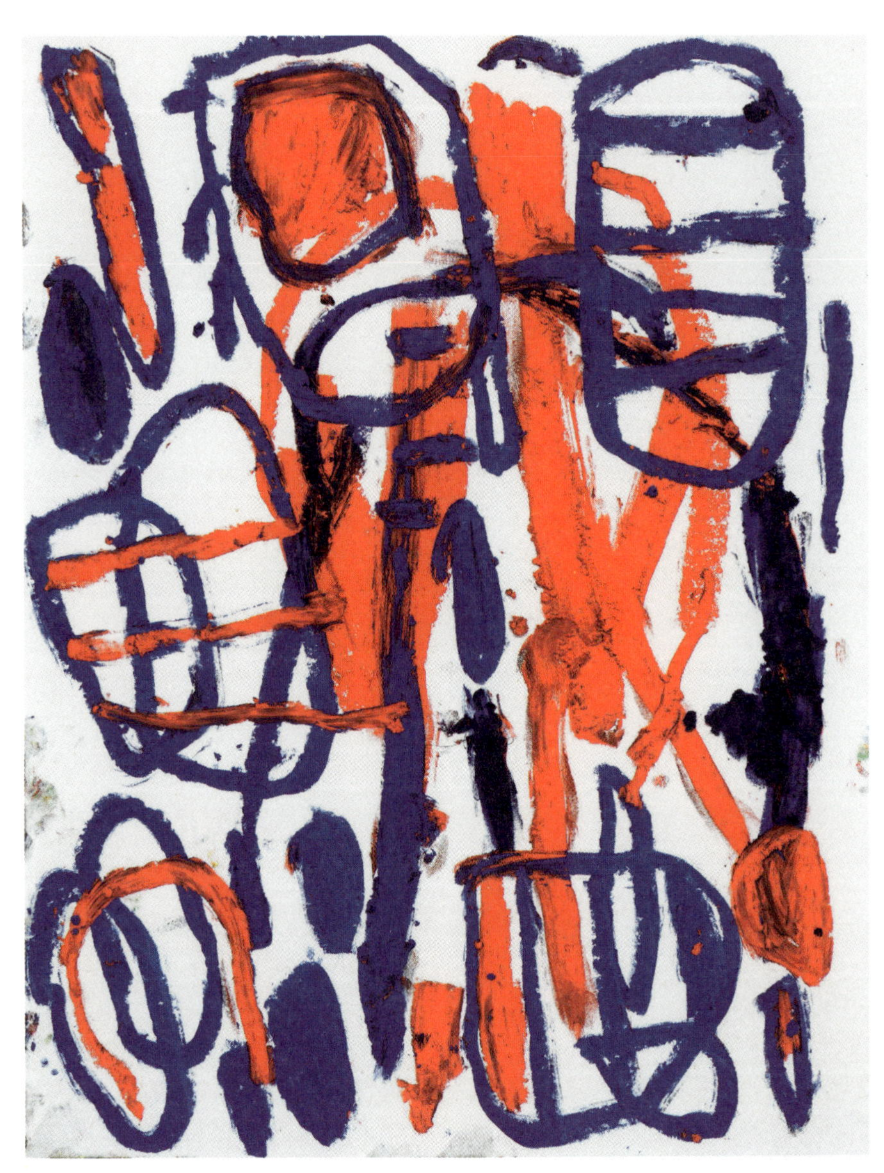

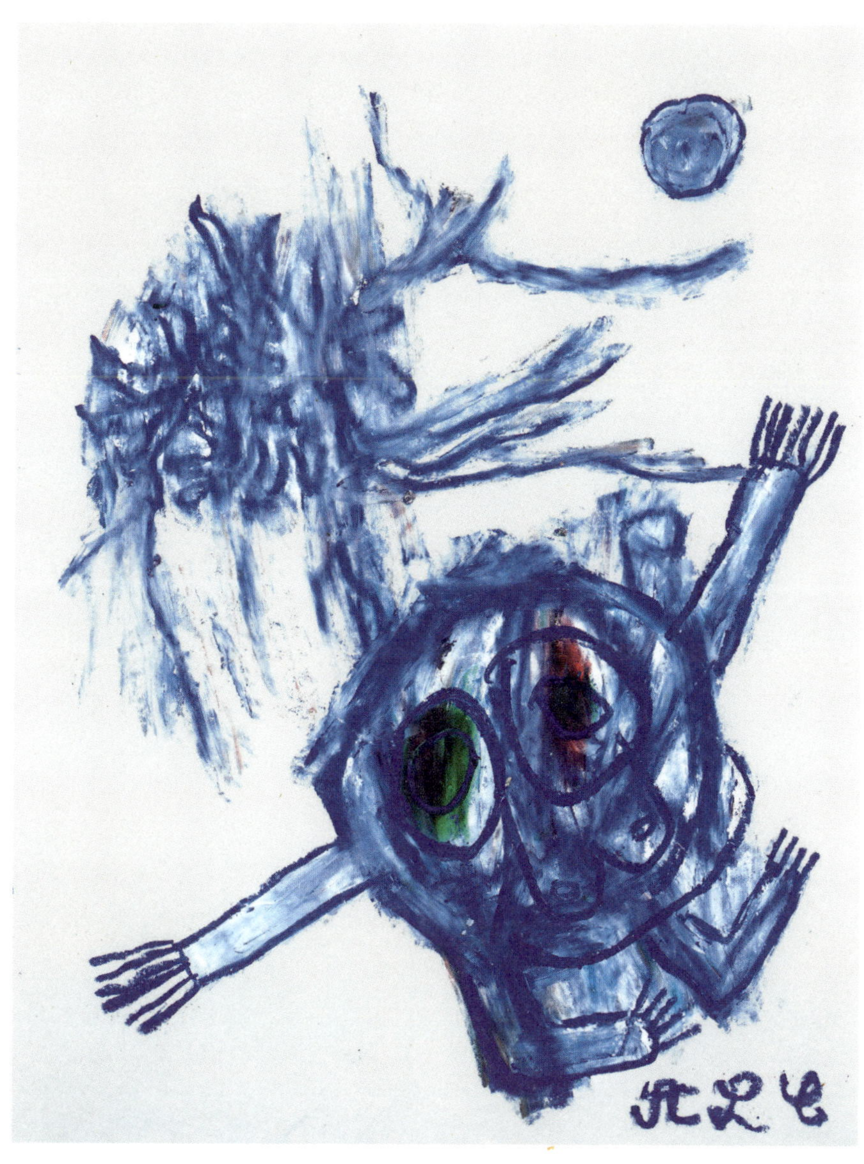

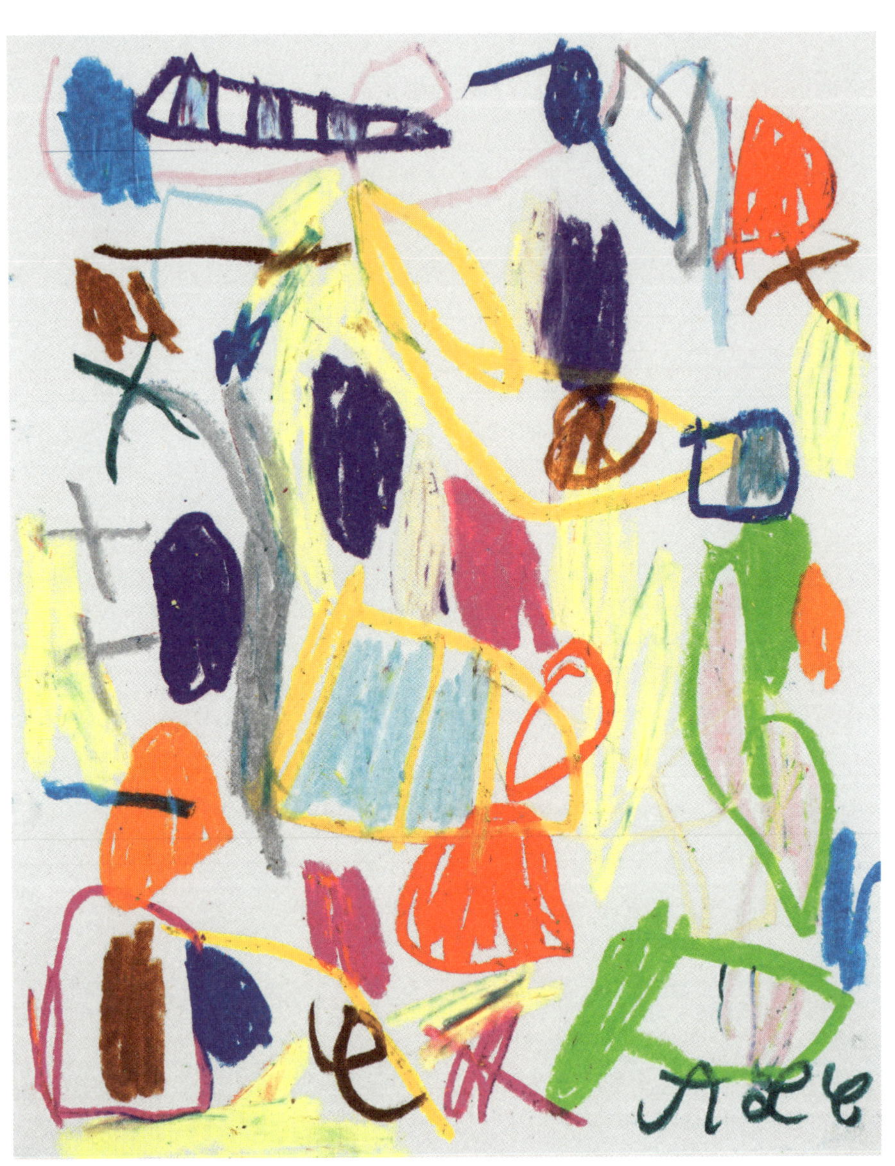

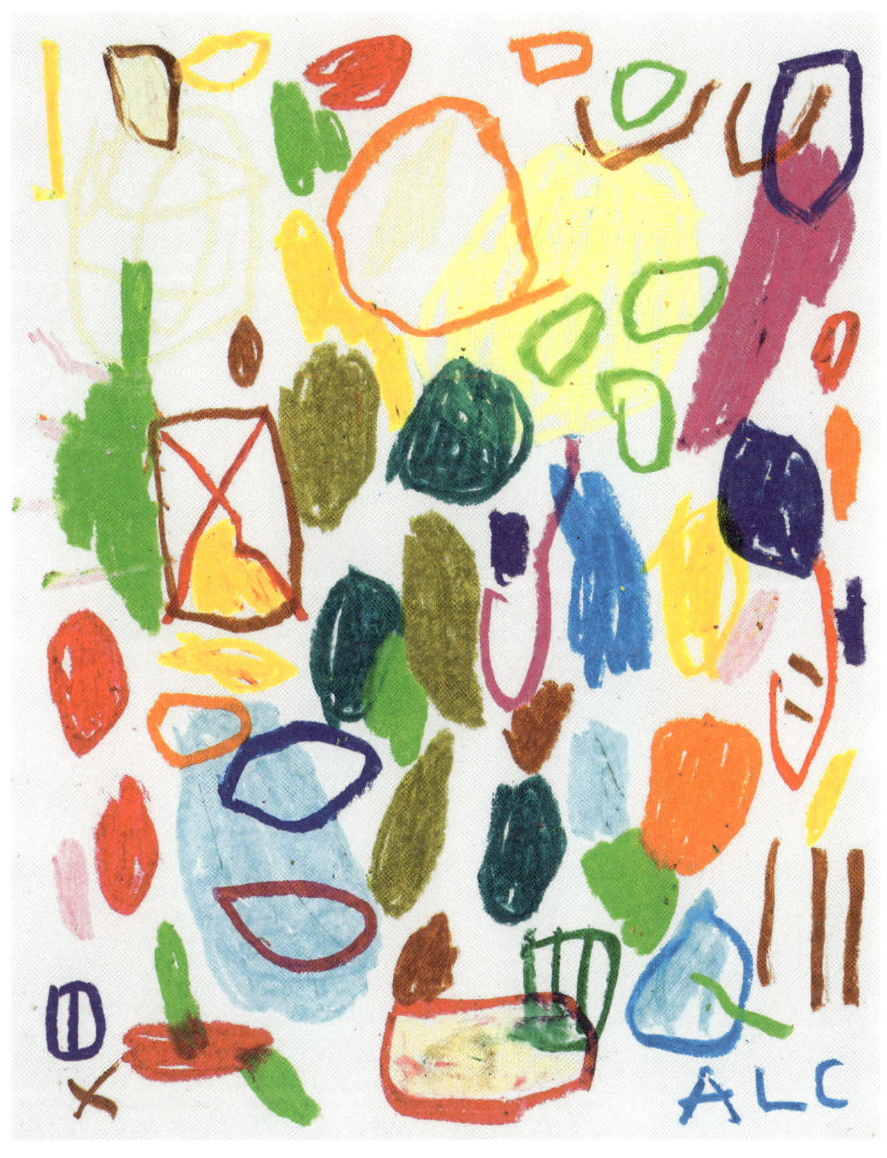
ALC

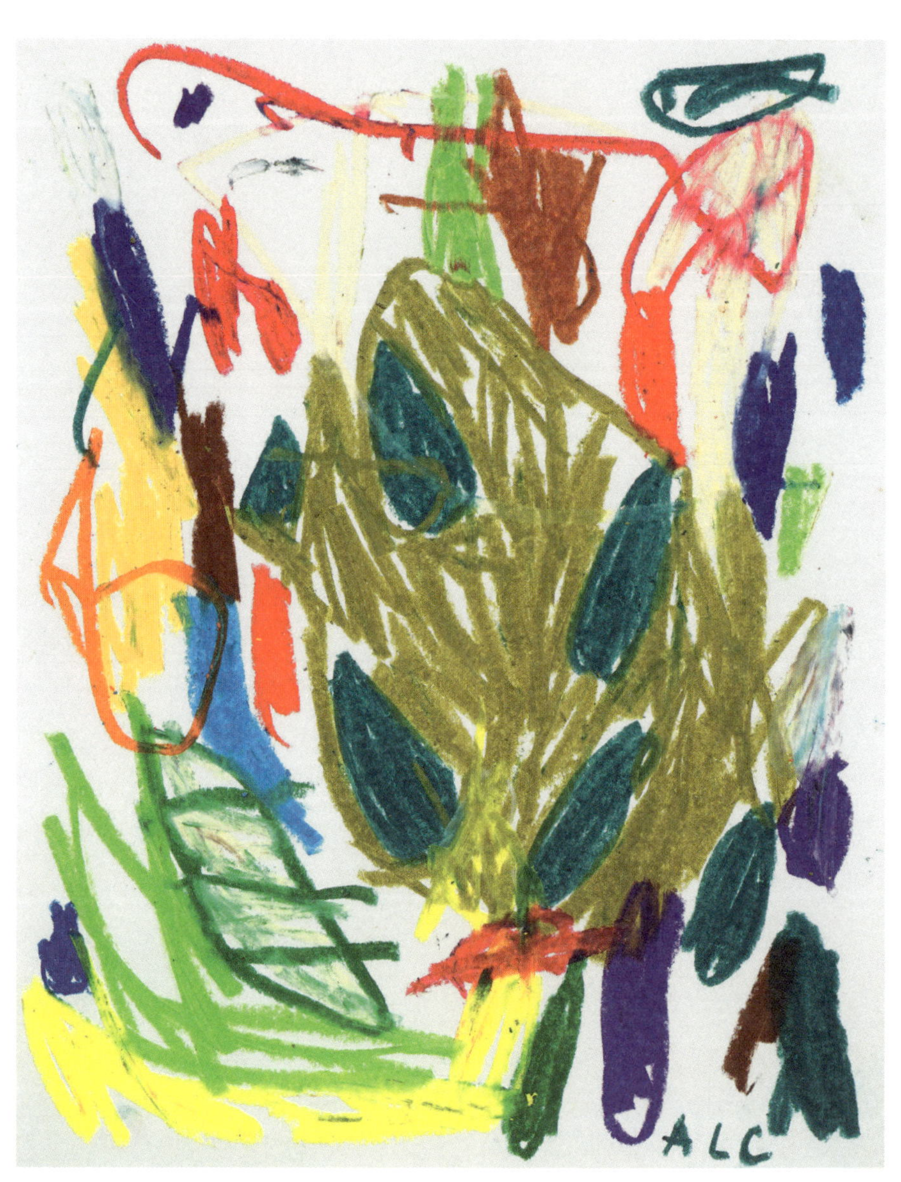
ALC

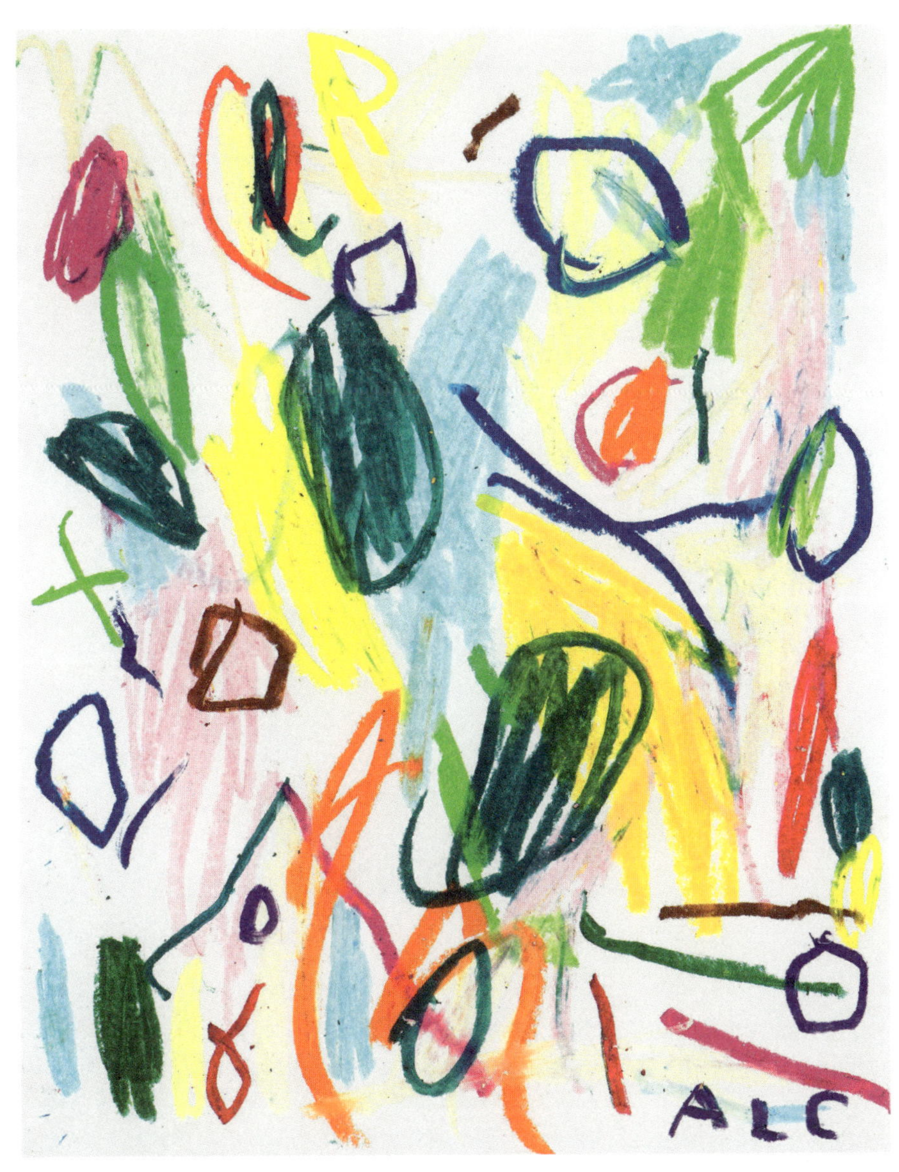
ALC

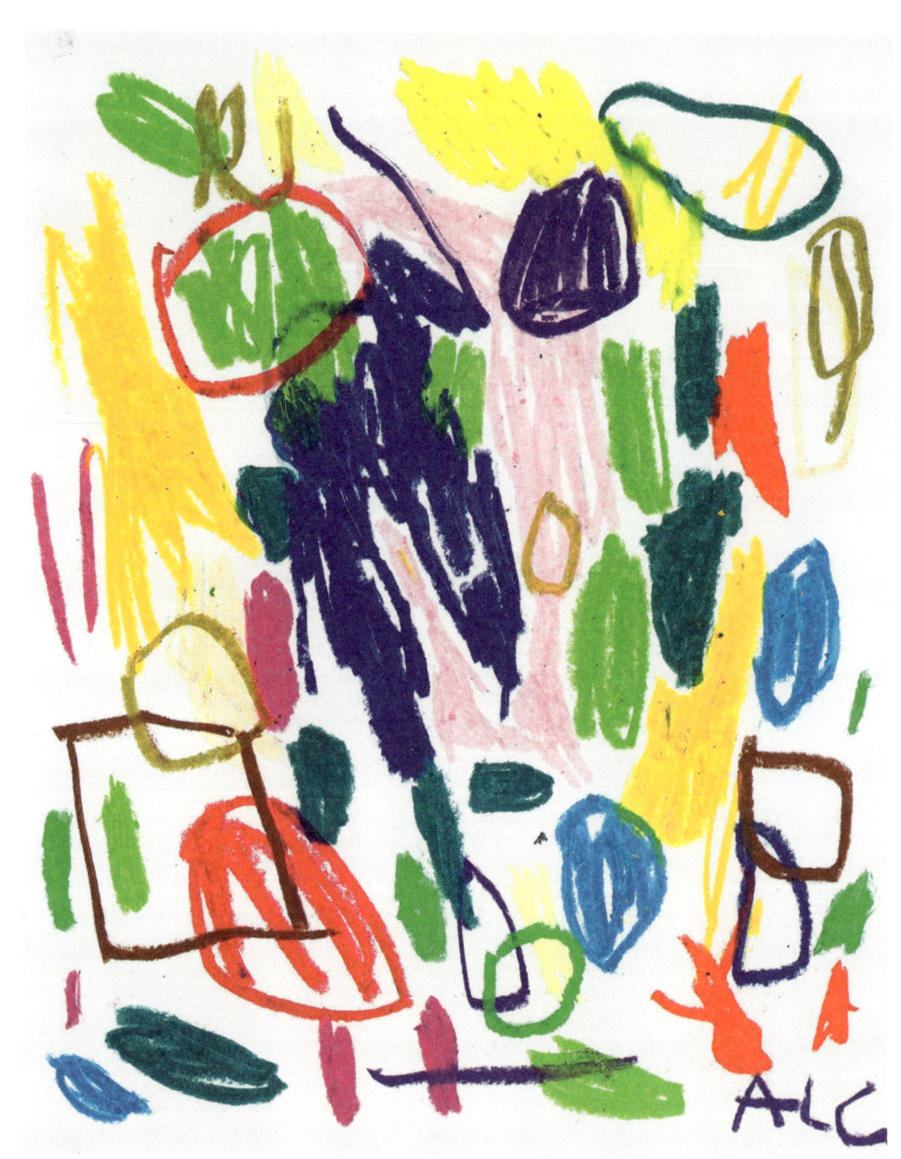
ALC

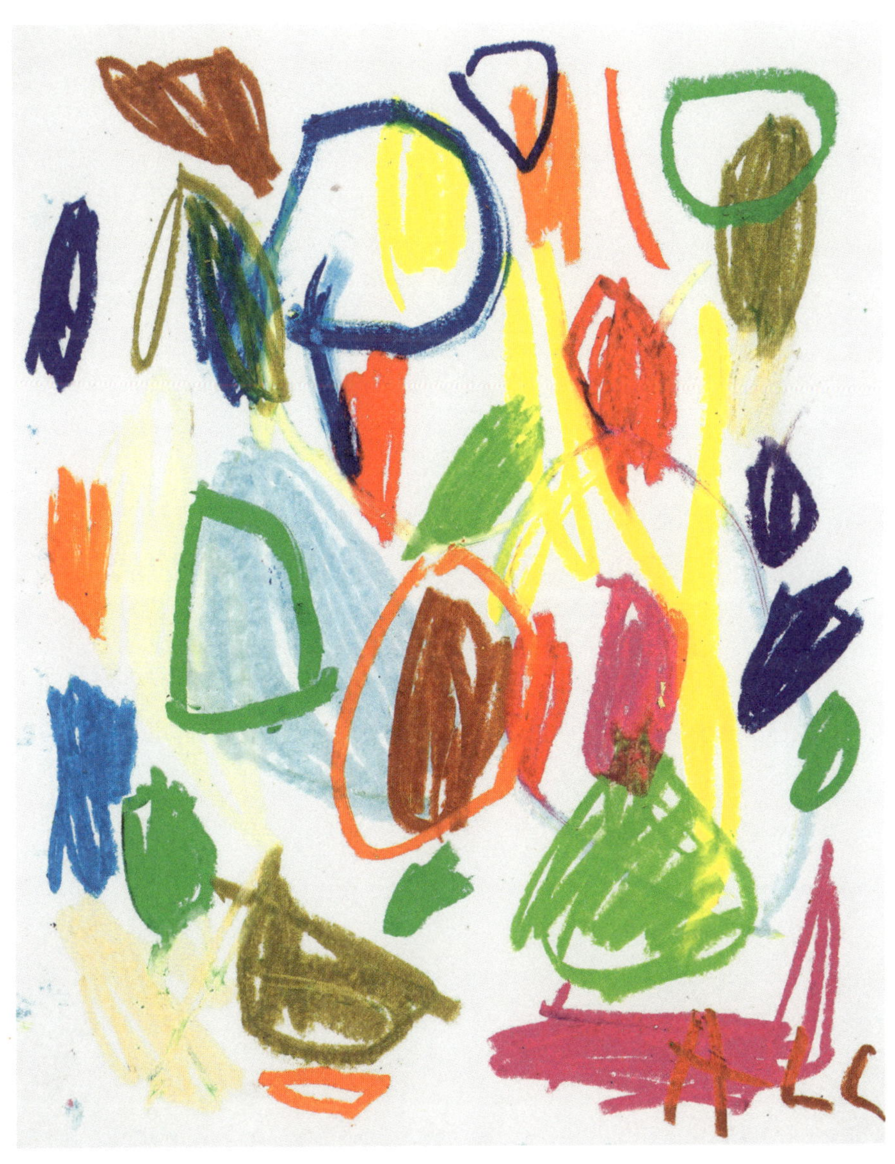
ALC

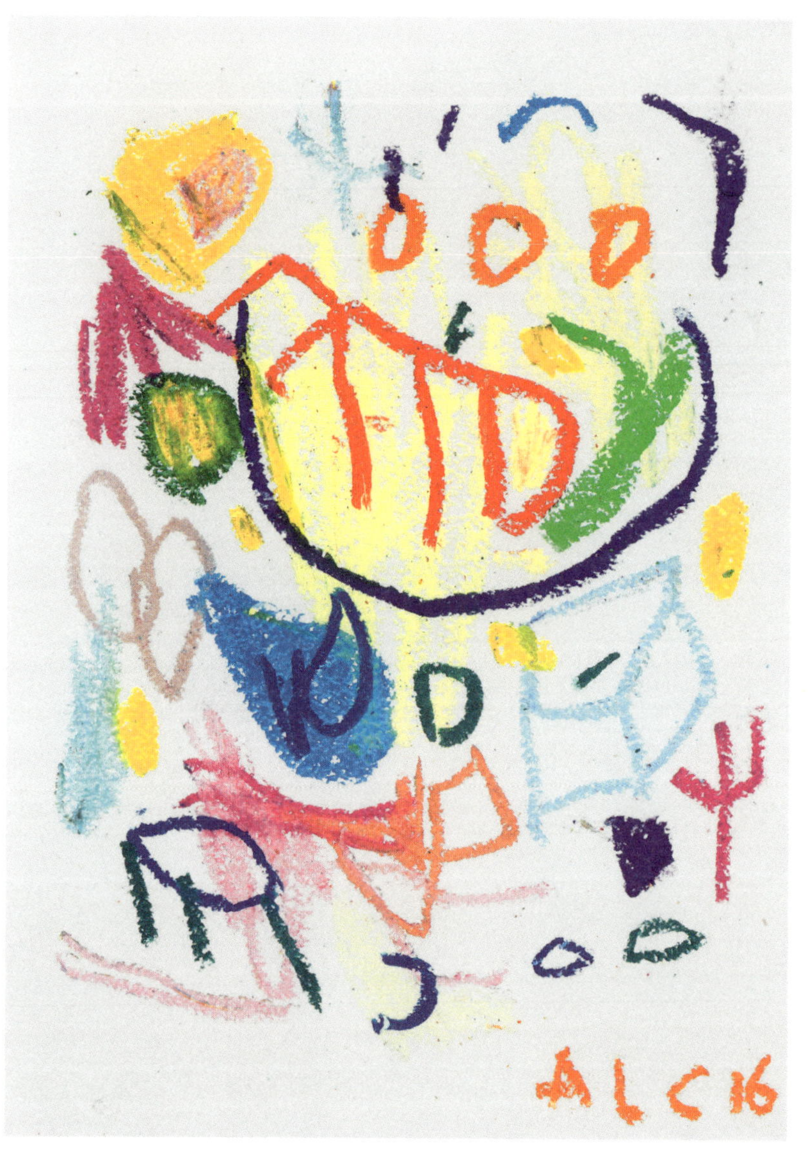
ALC16

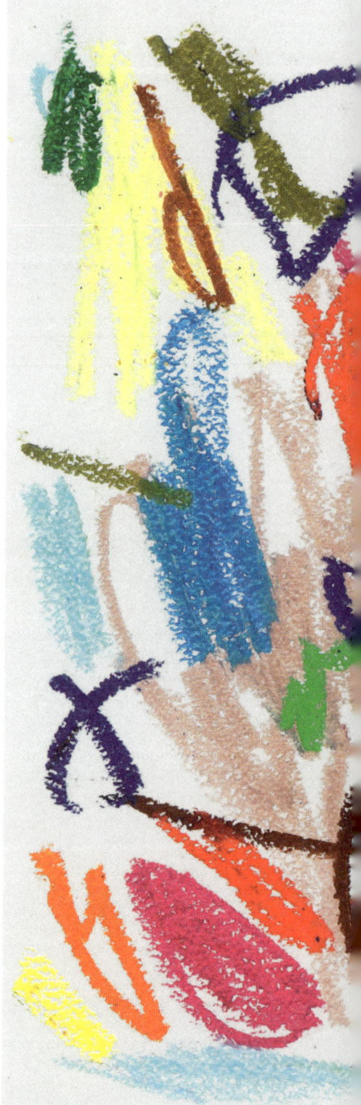

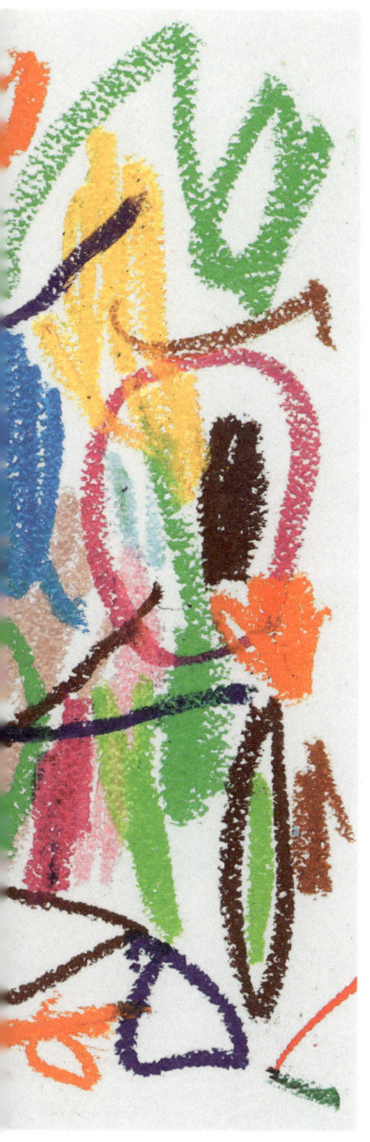

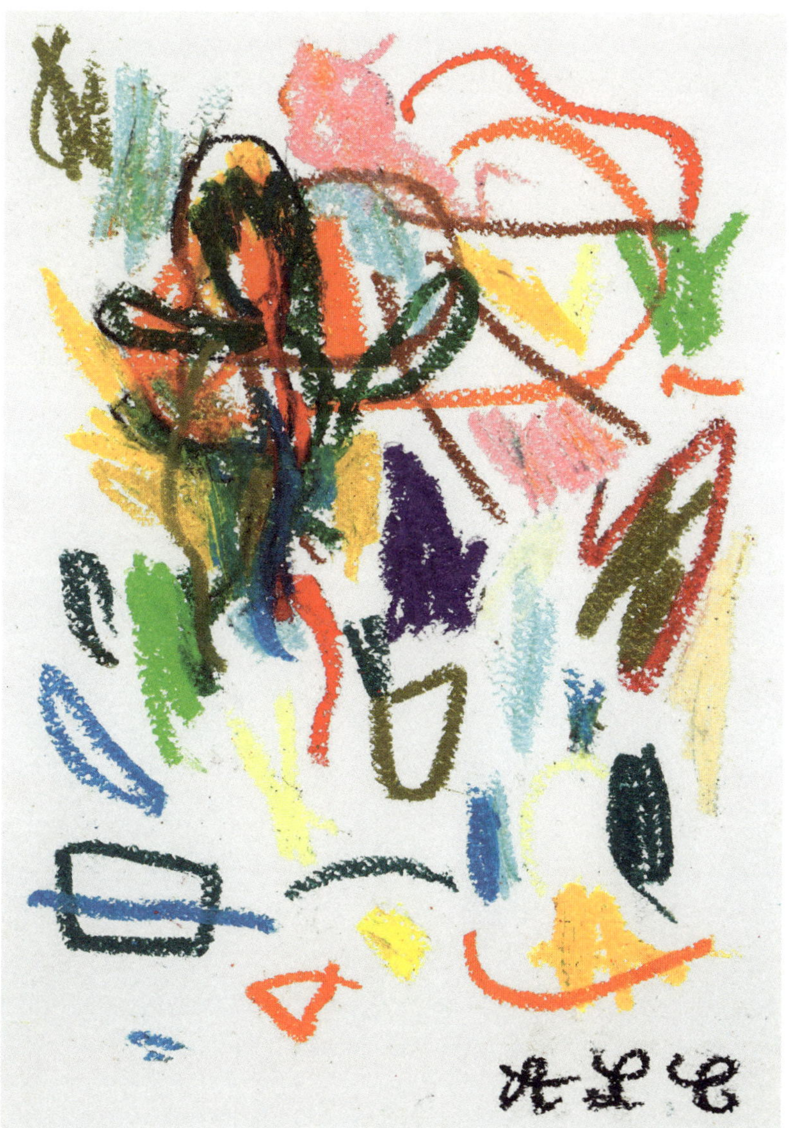

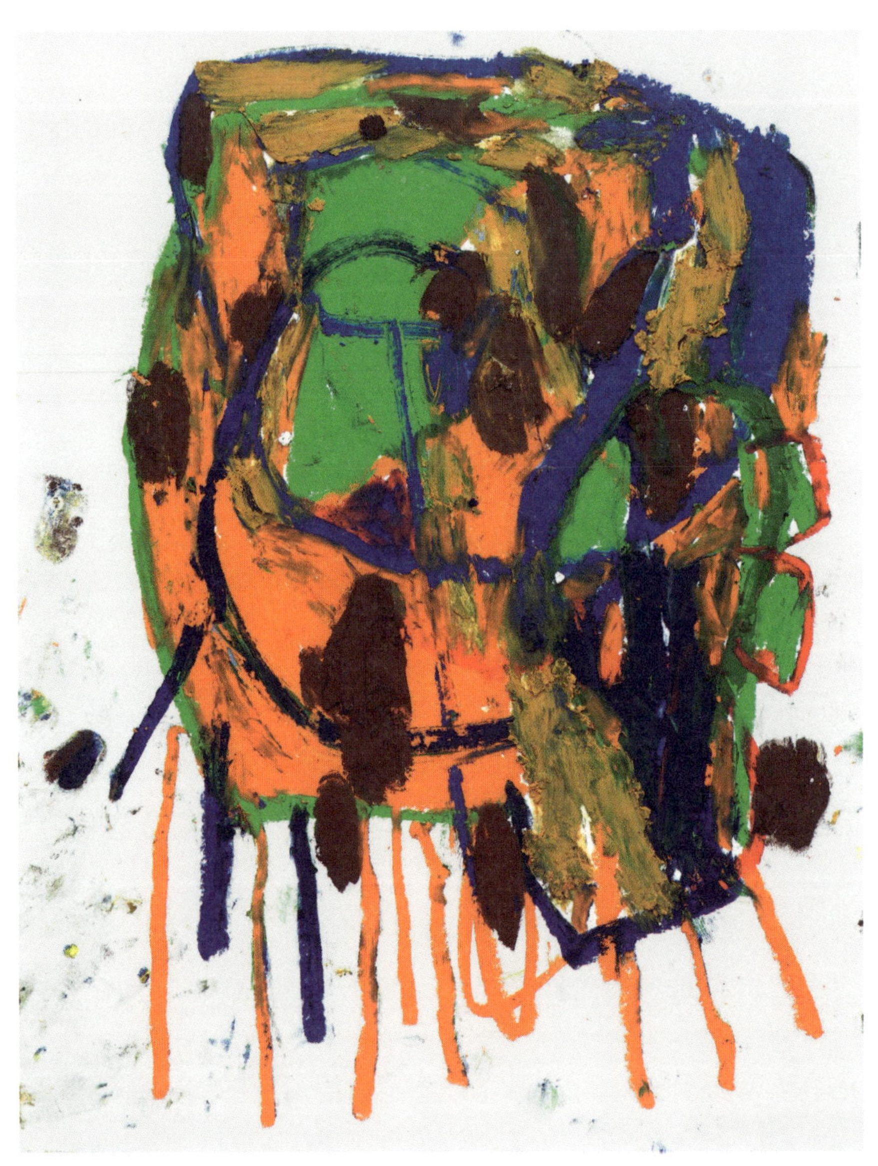

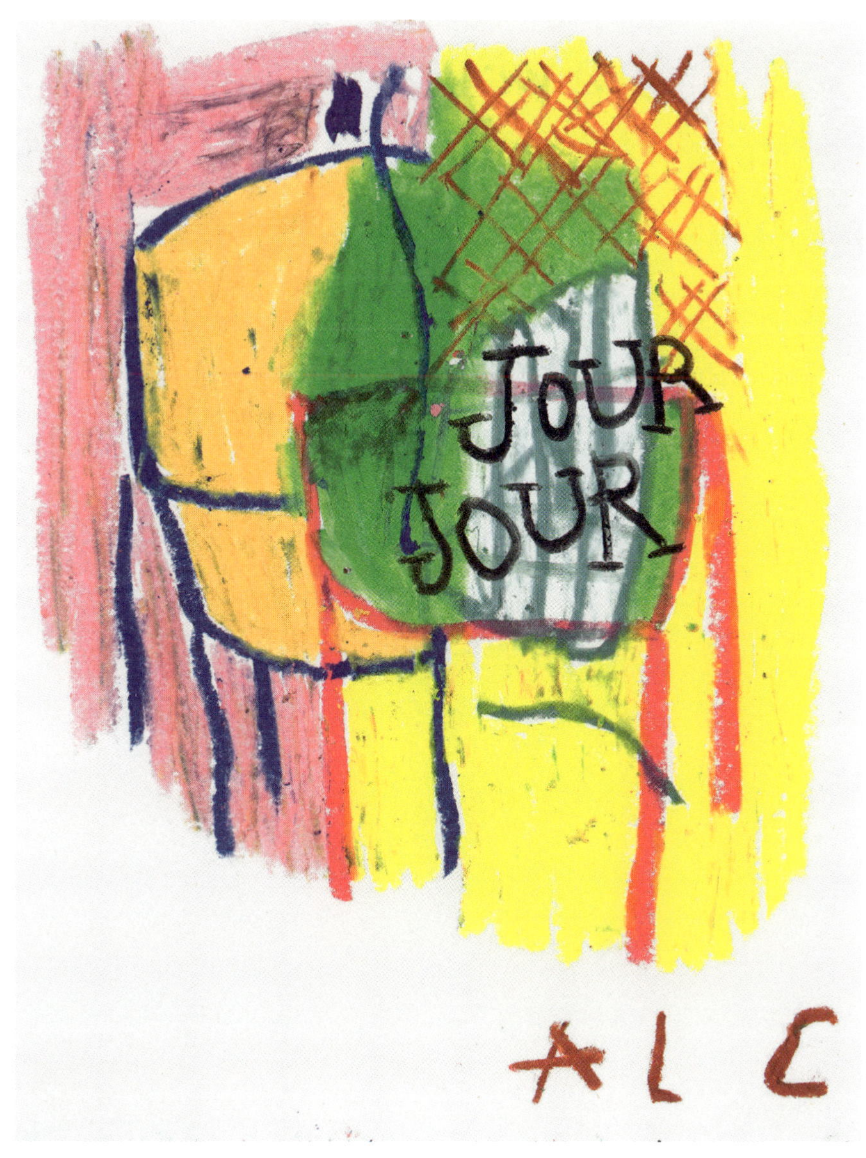
JOUR
JOUR
ALC

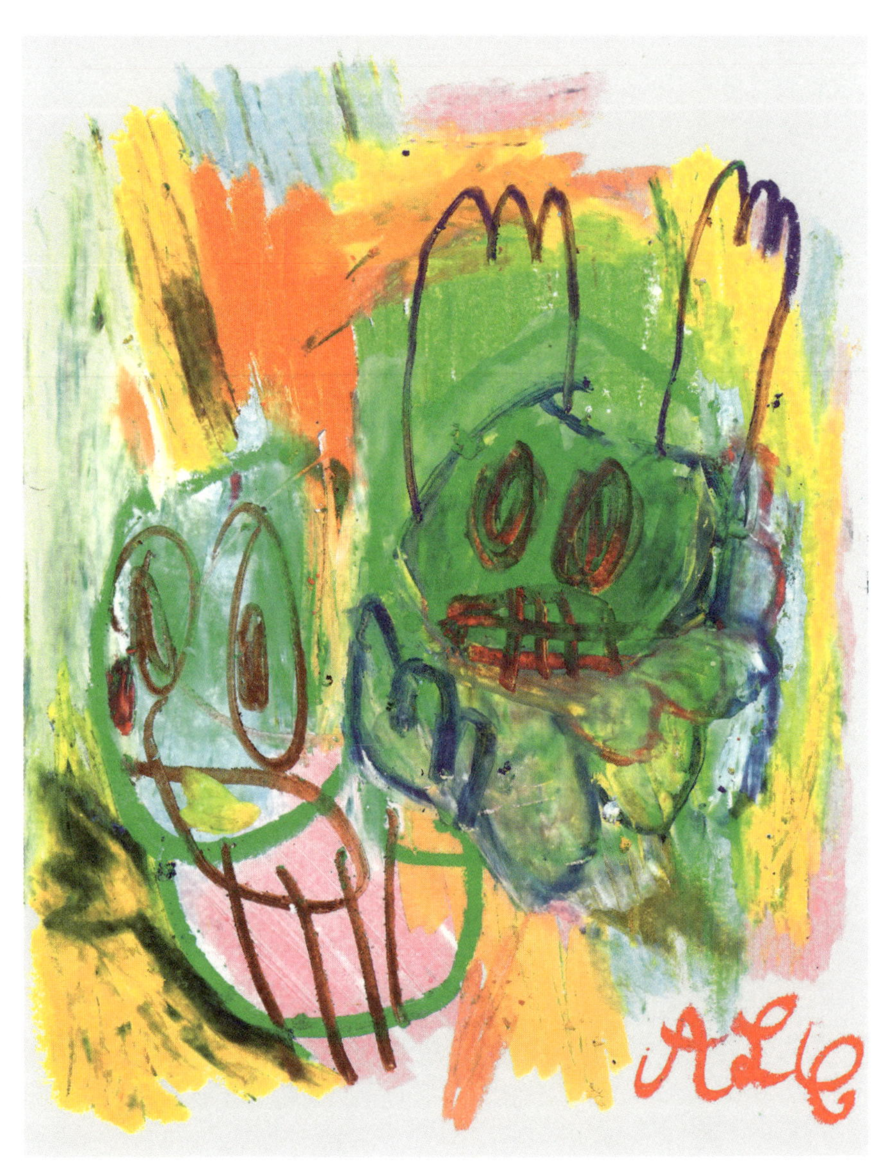
ALC

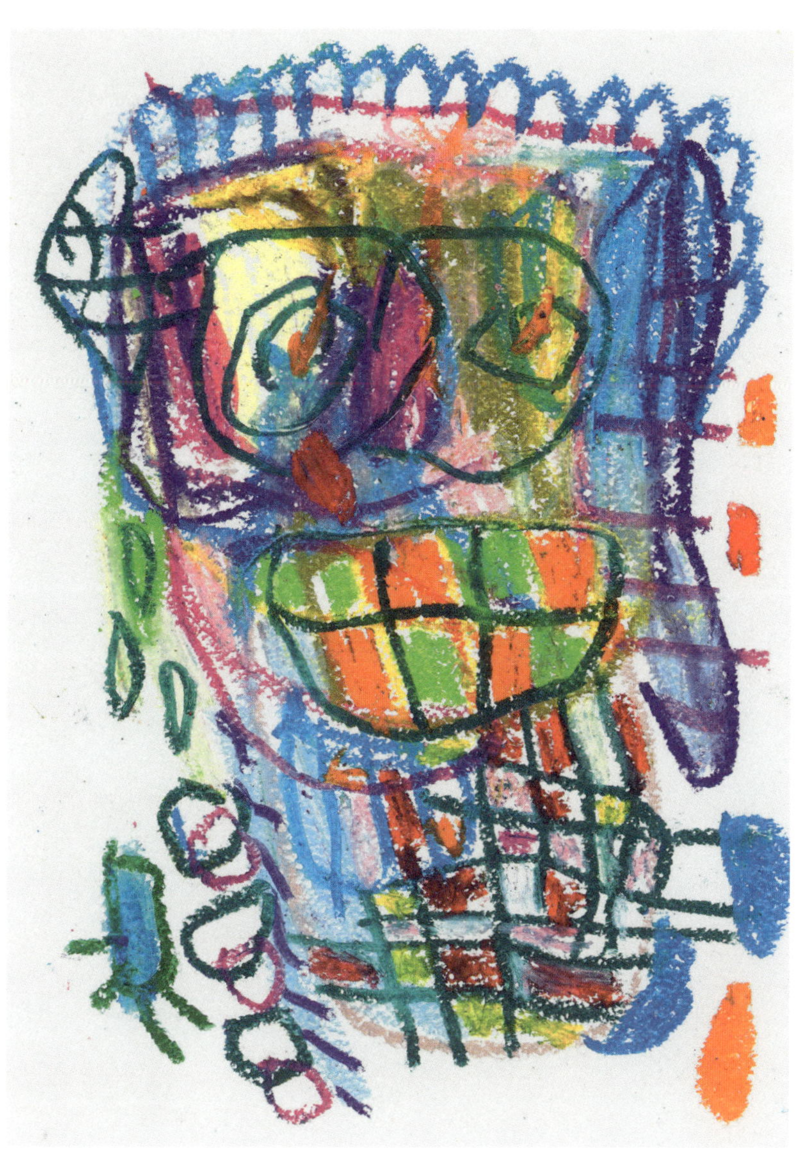

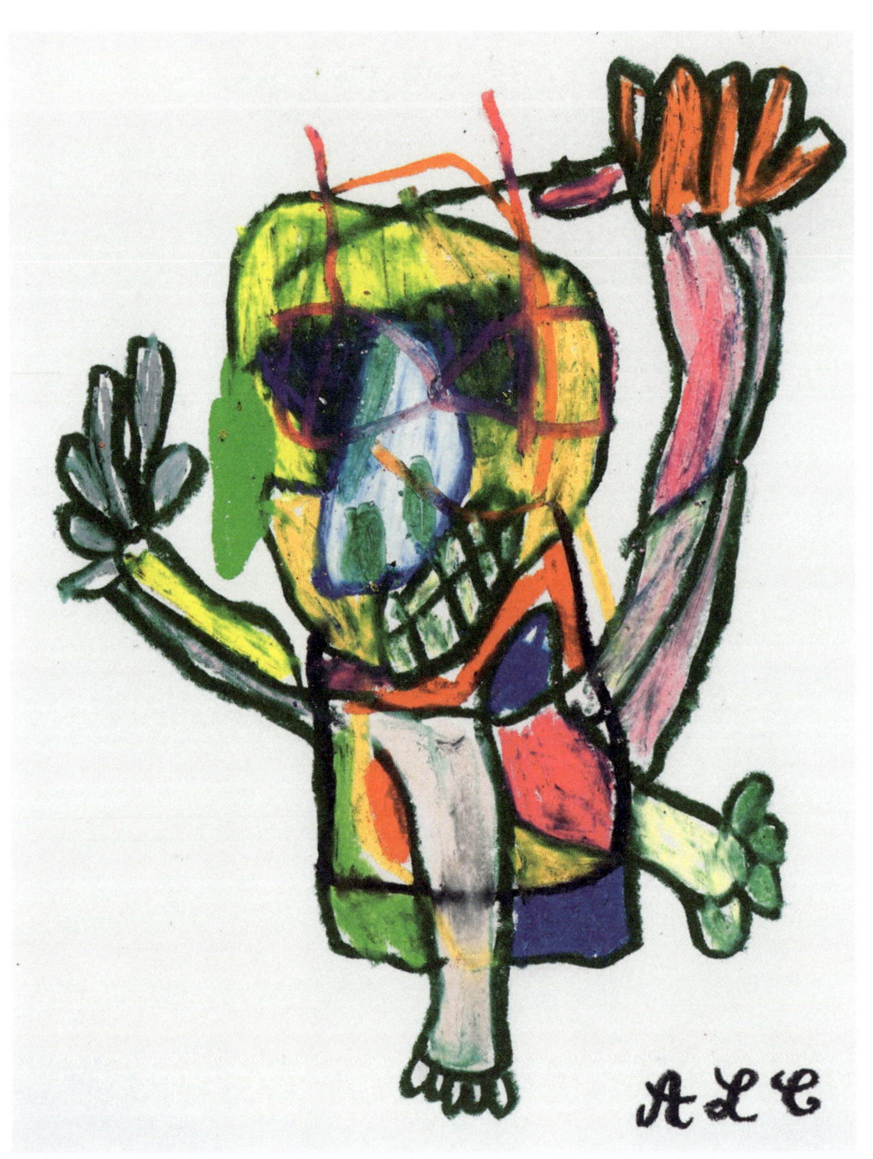
ALC

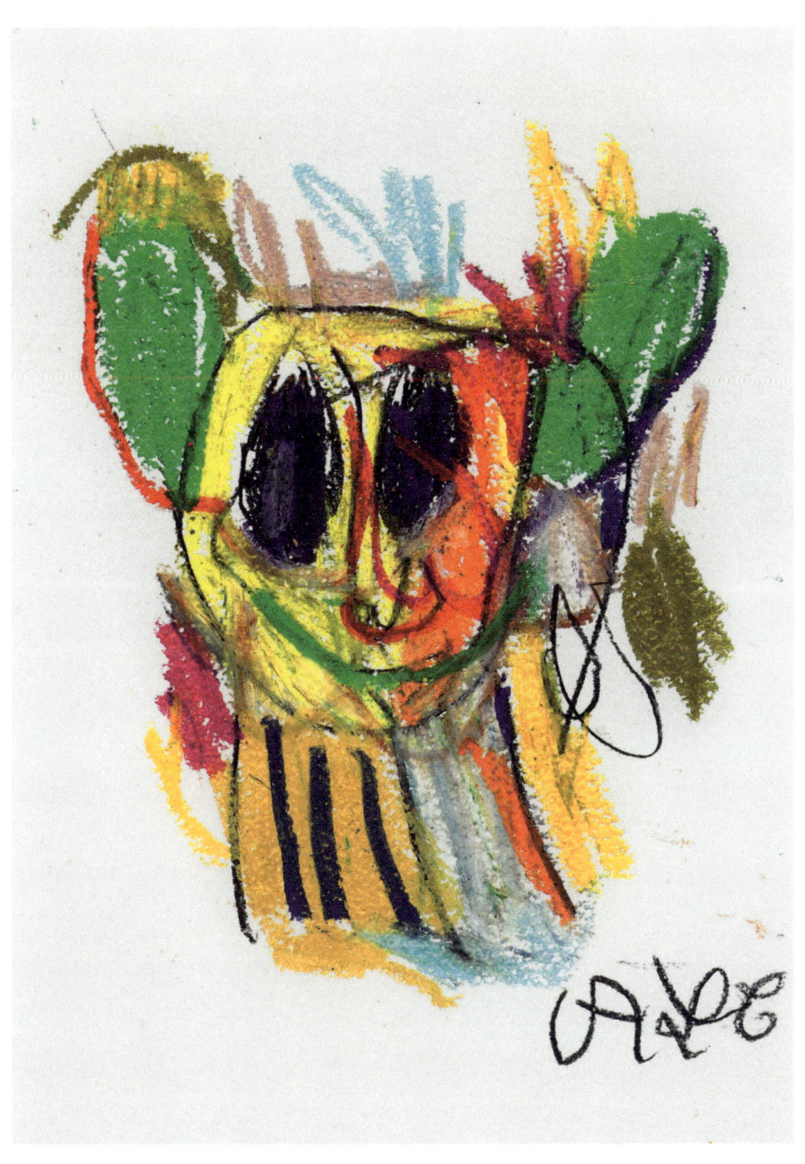

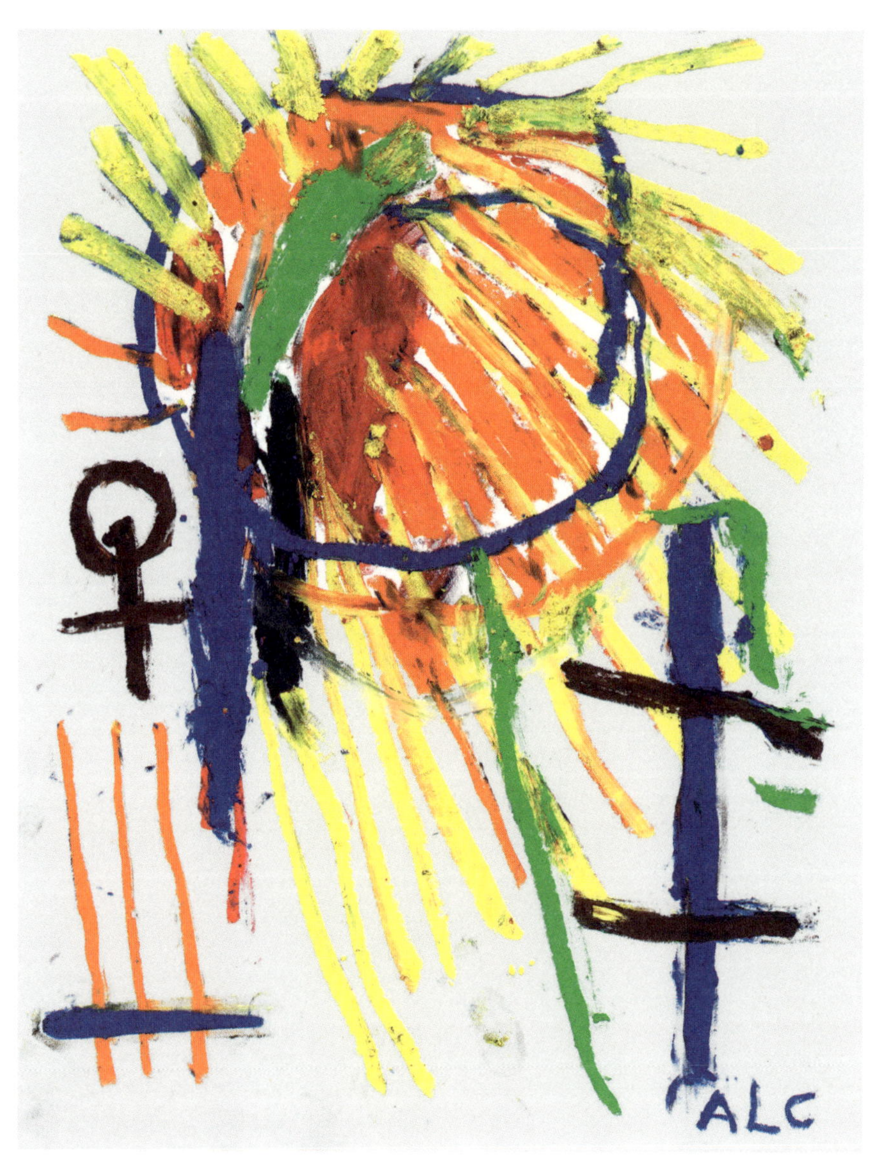
ALC

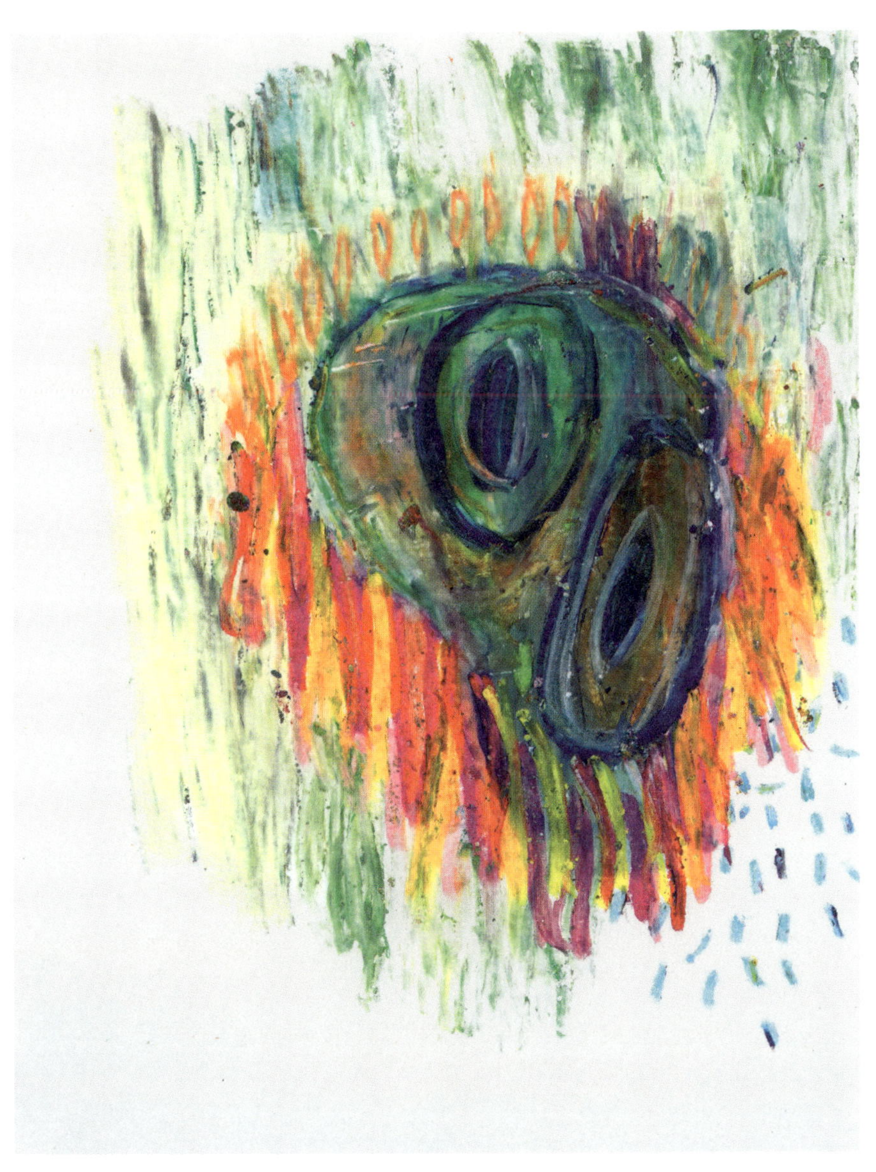

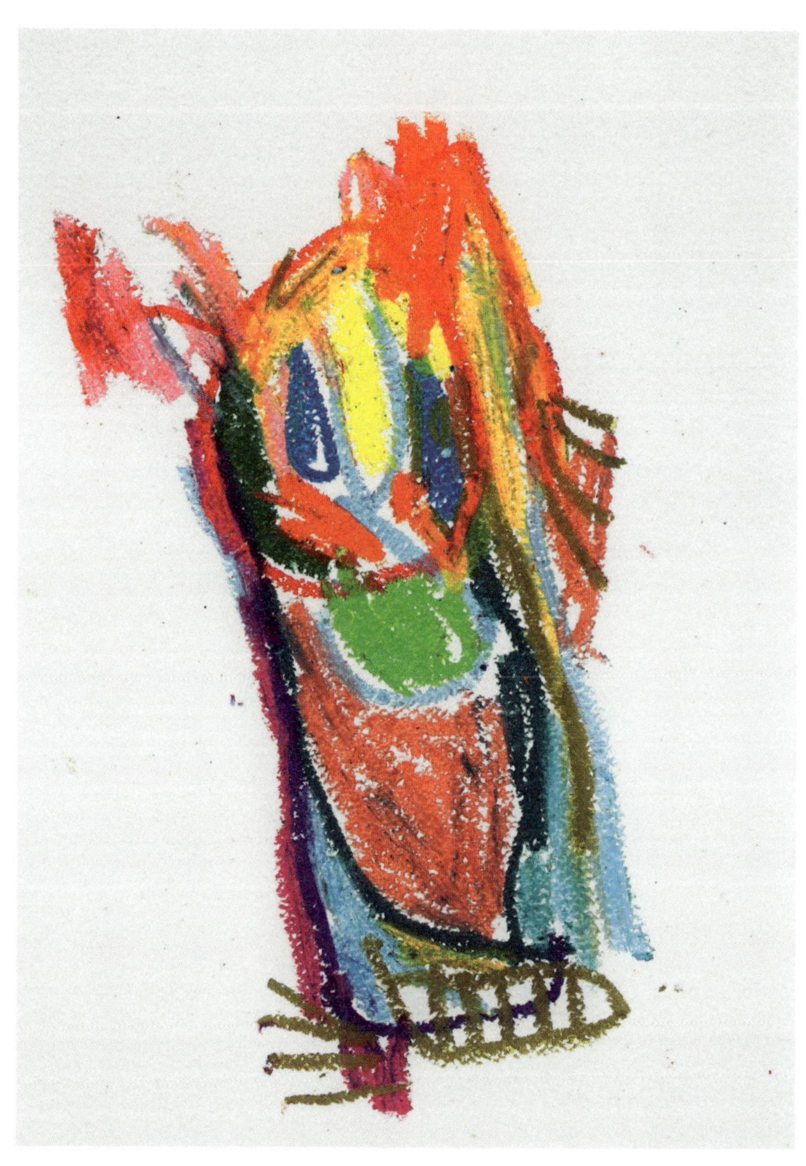

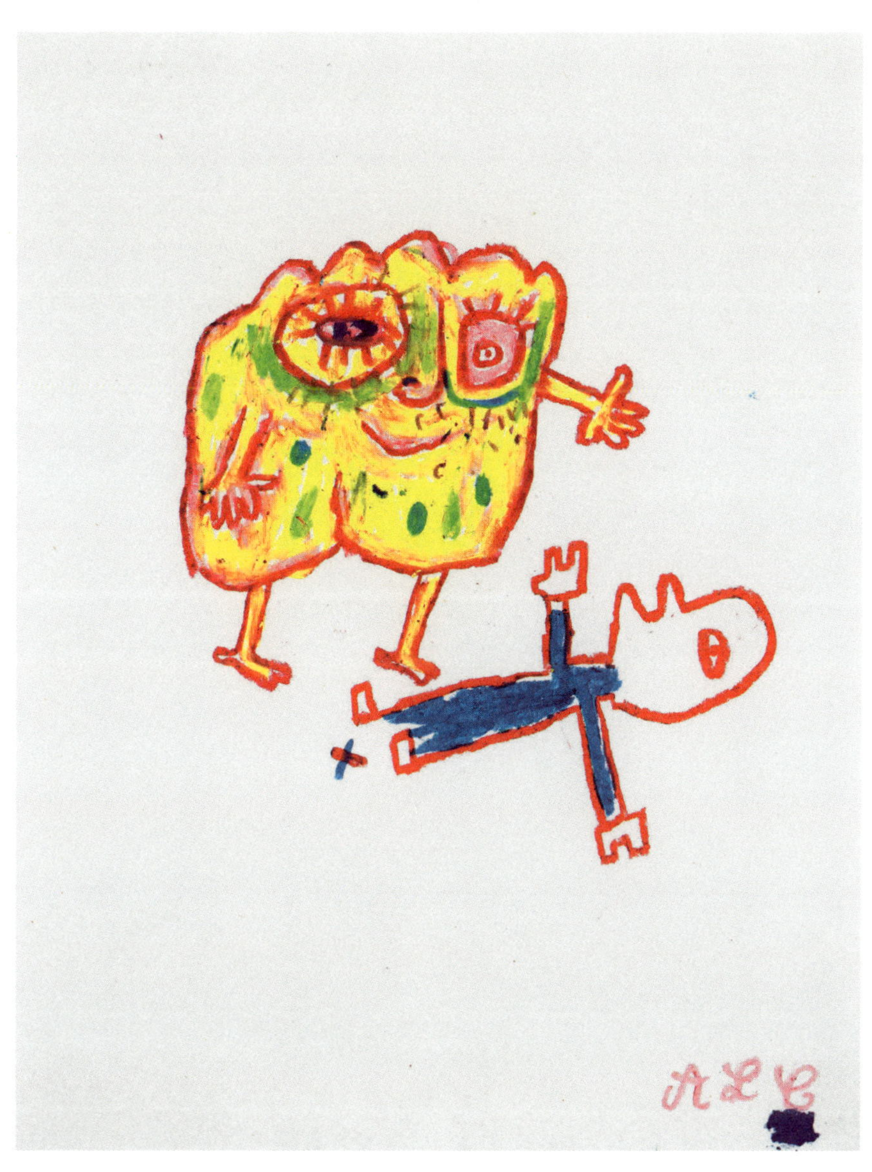
ALC

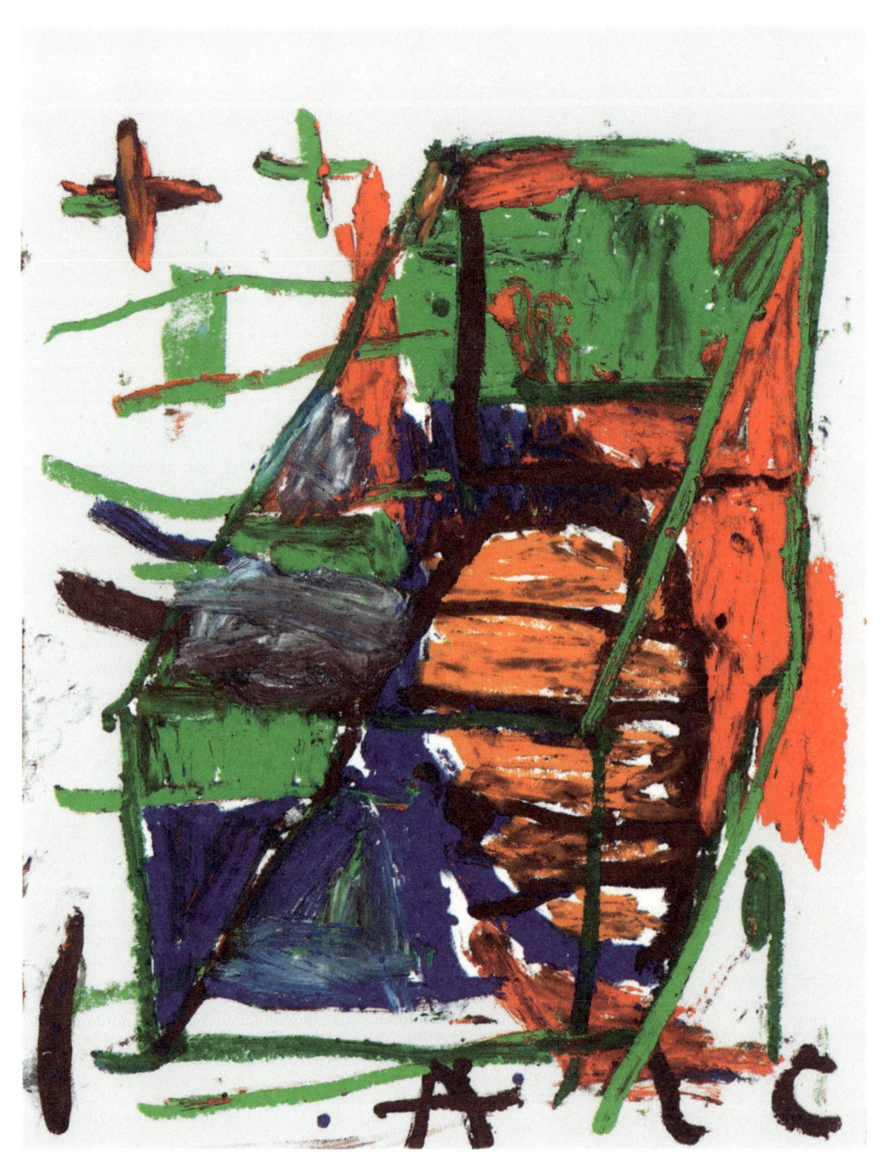

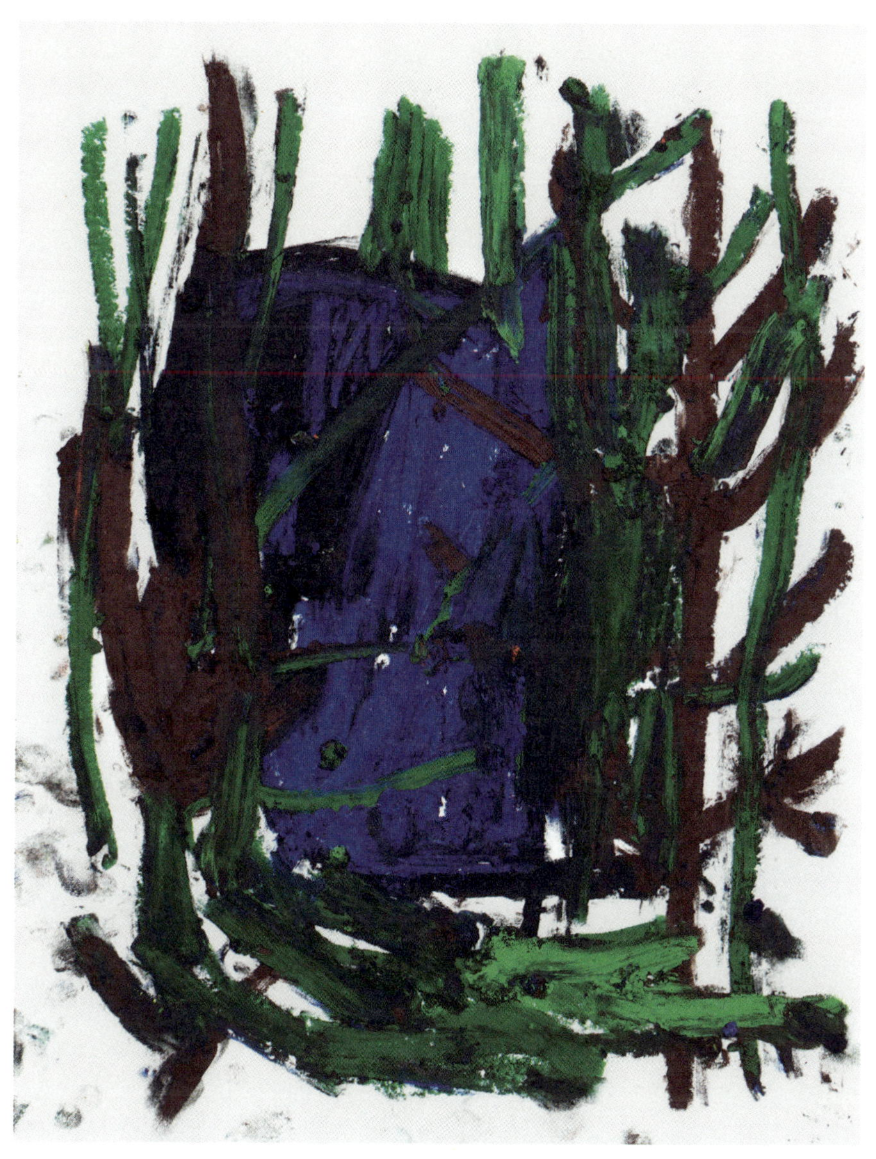

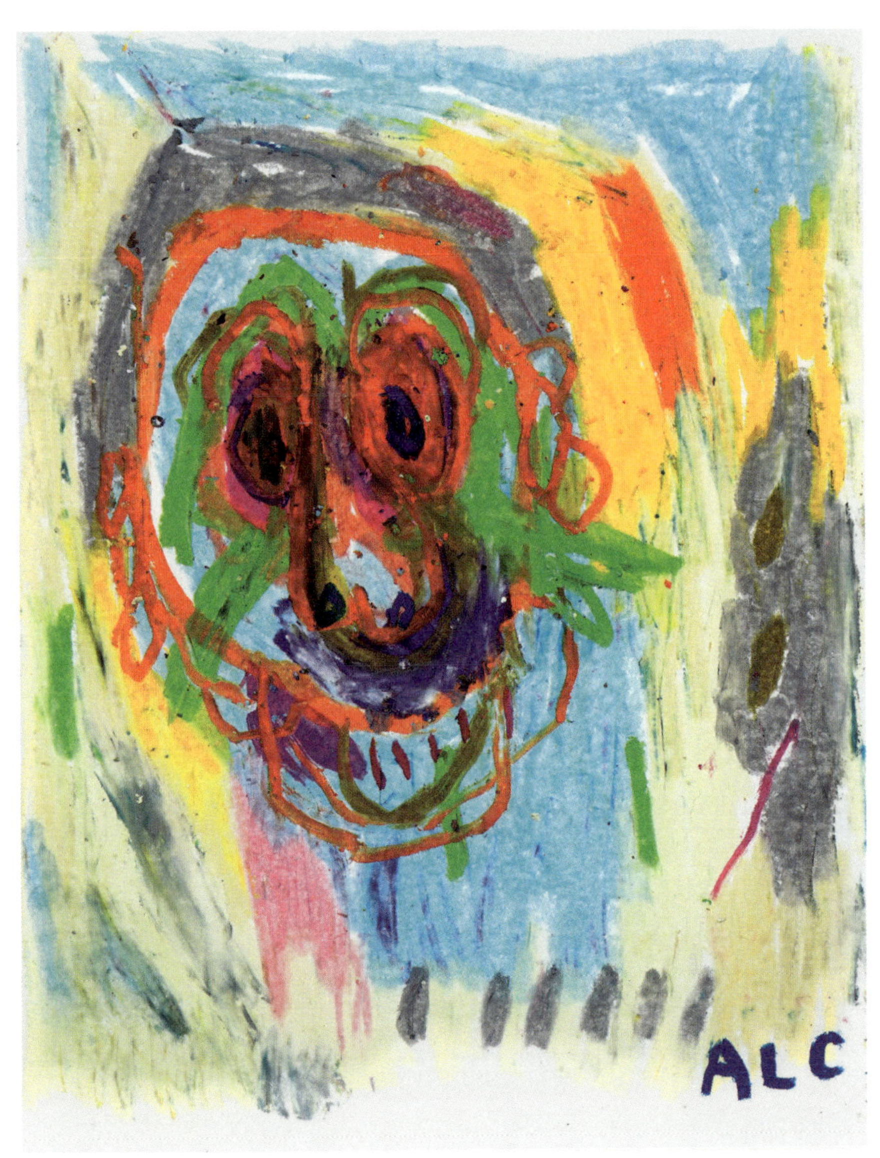
ALC

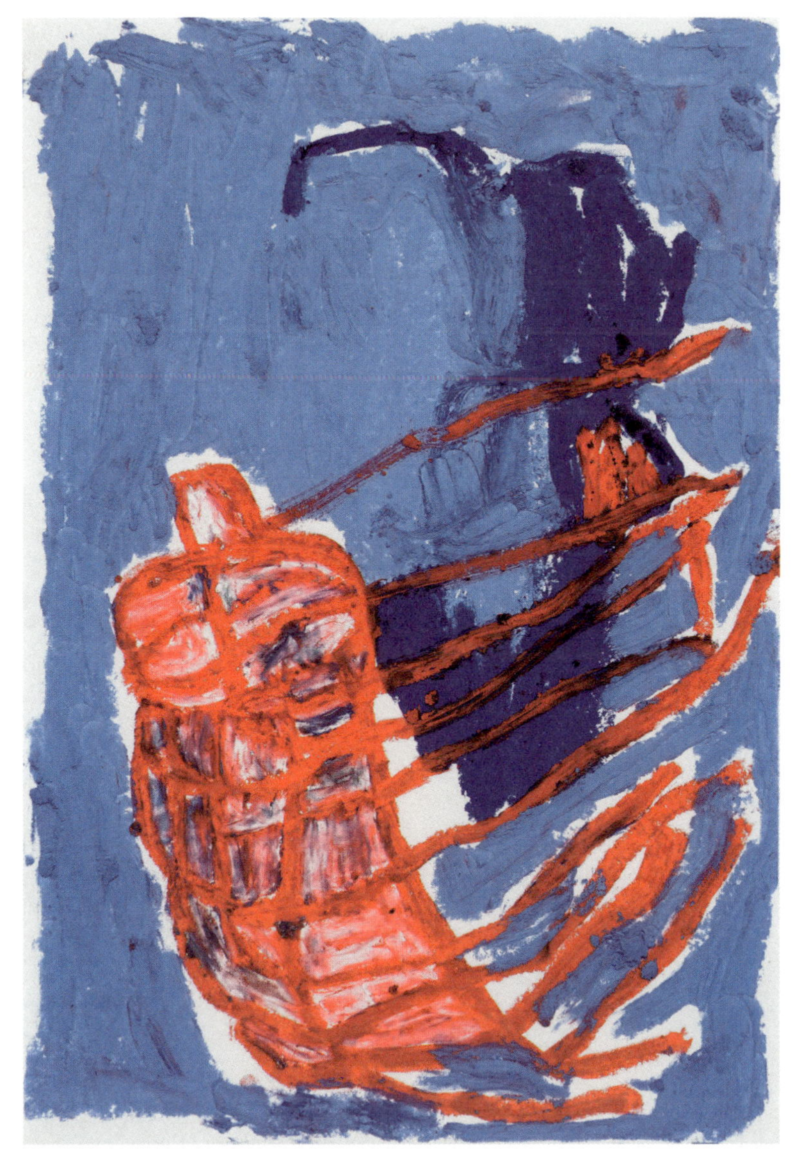

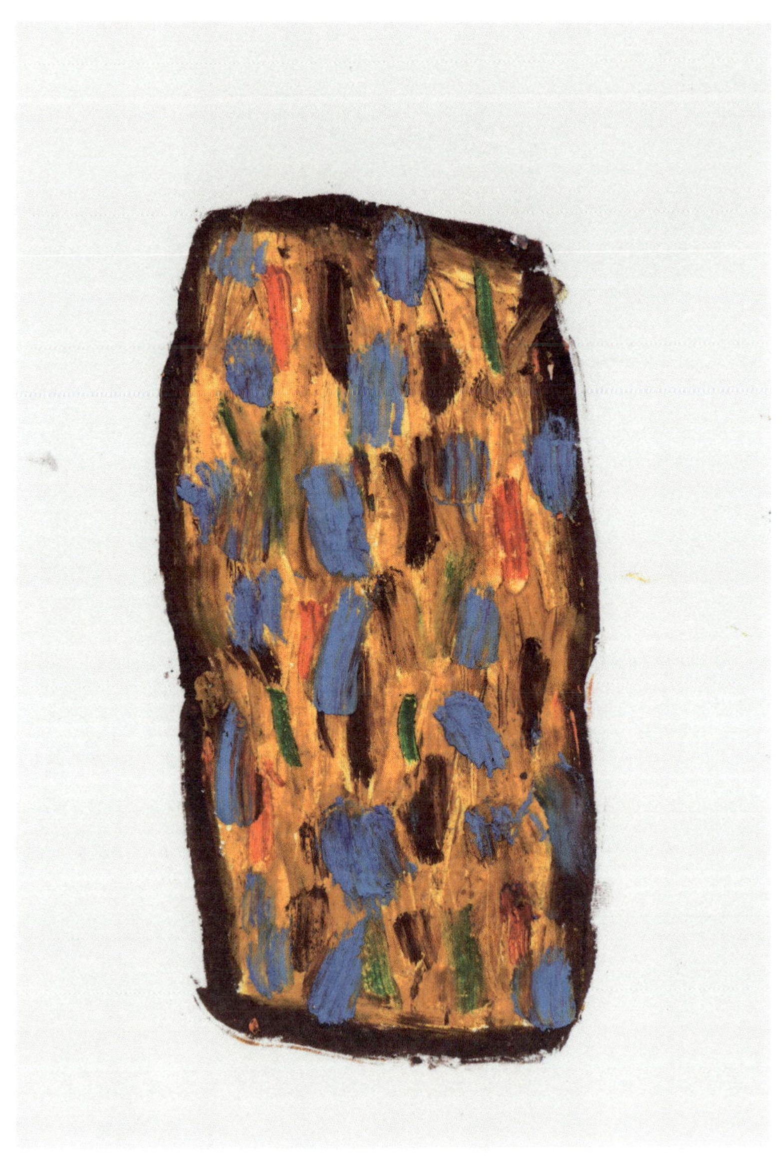

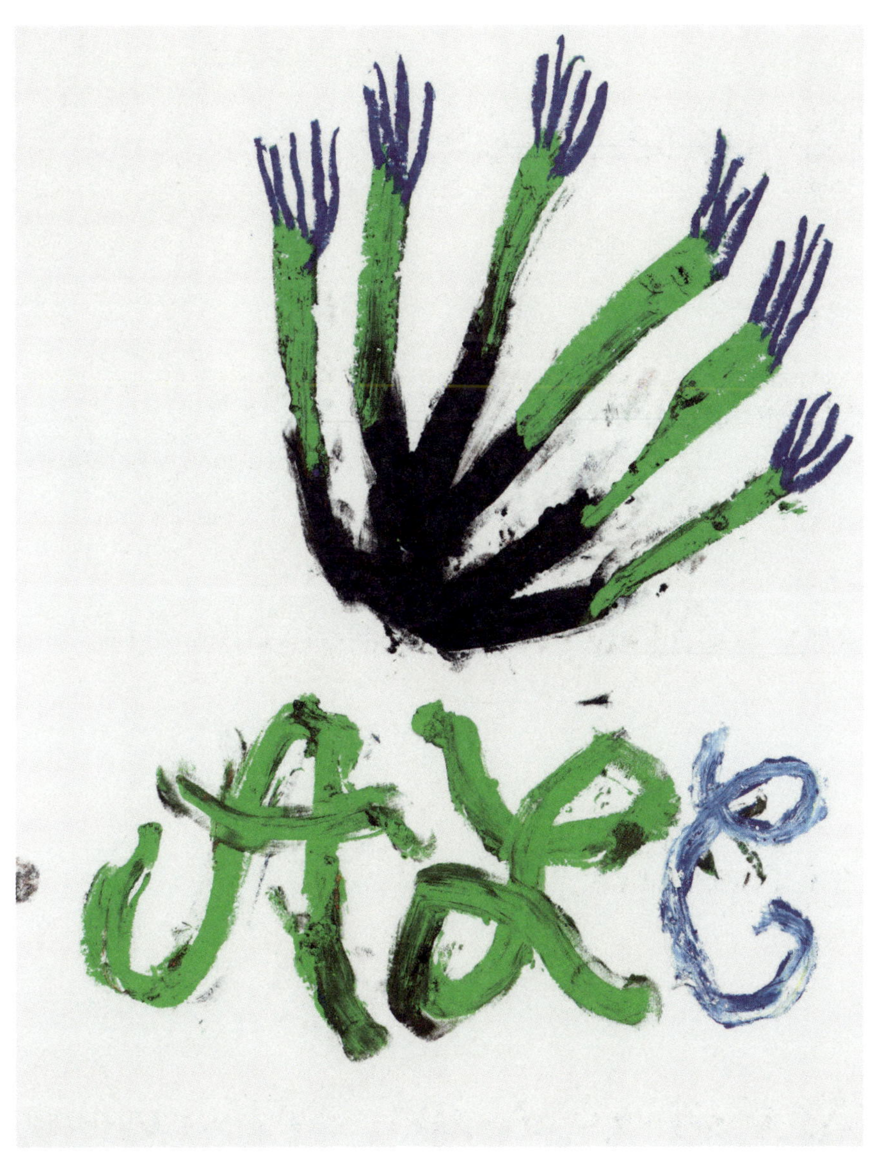

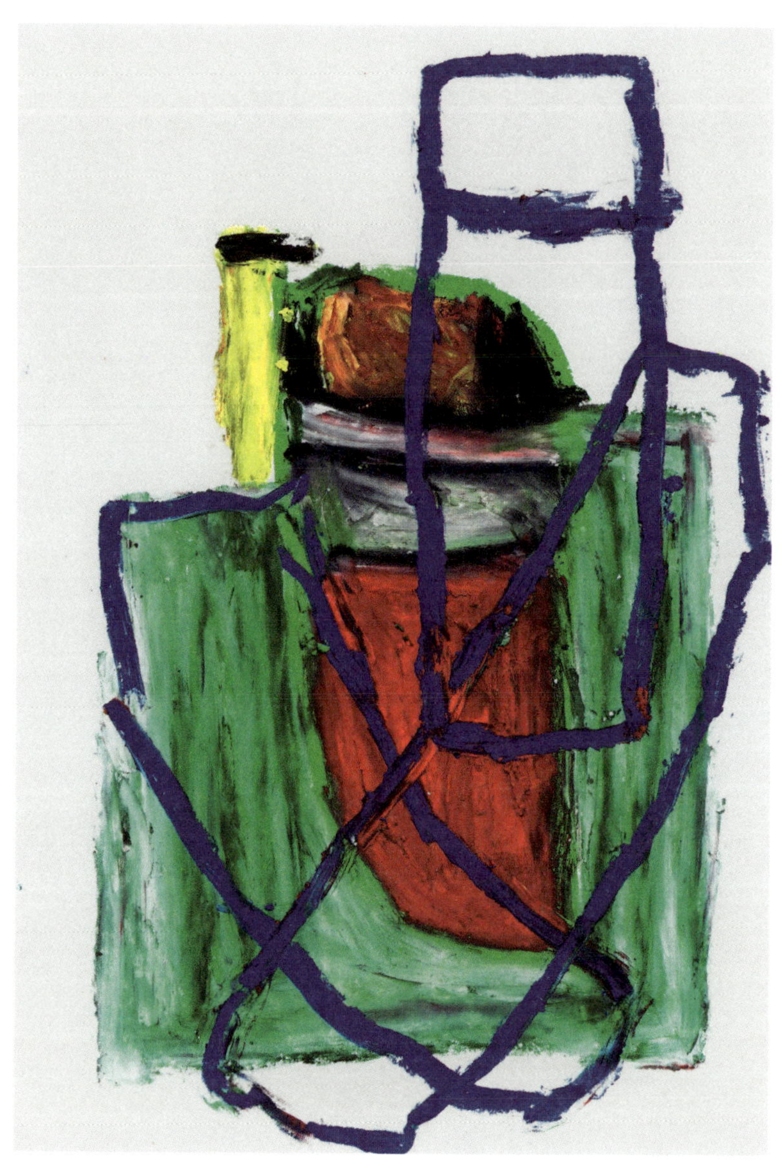

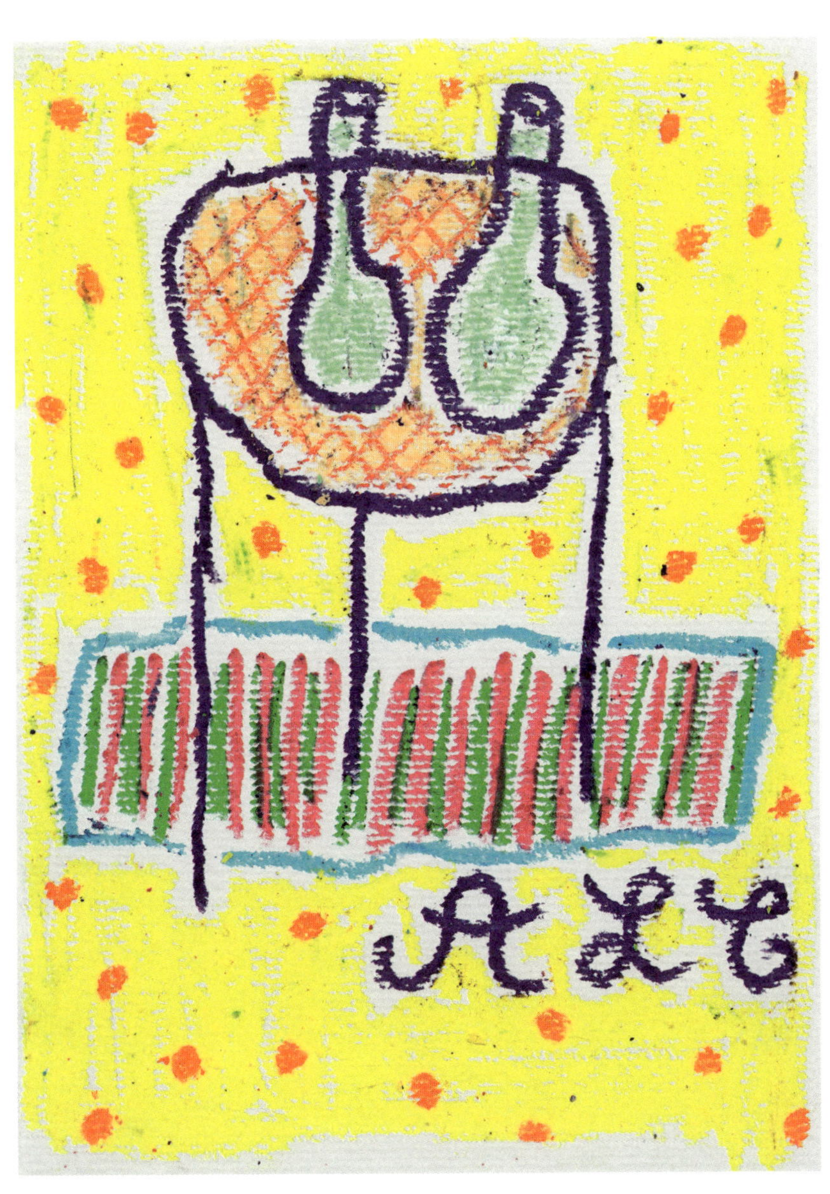
ALC

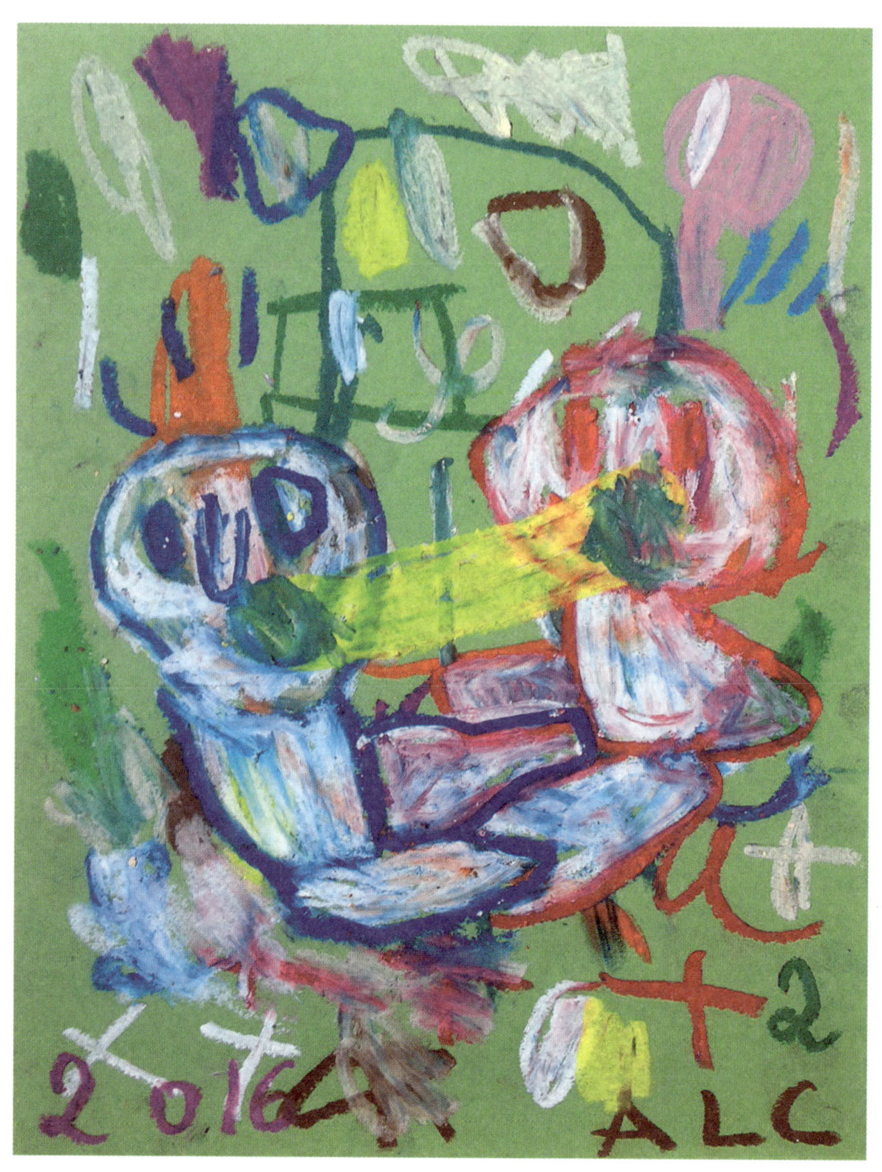
2016
ALC

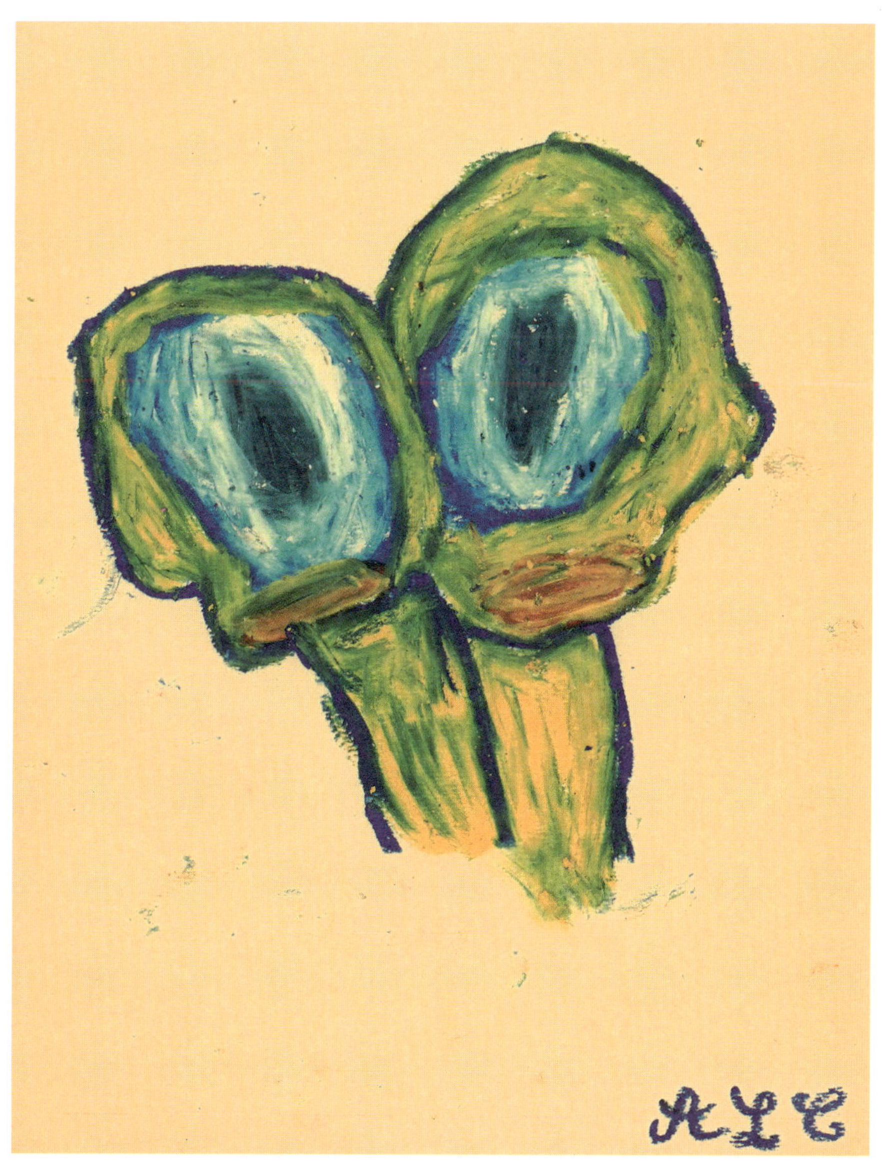
ALC

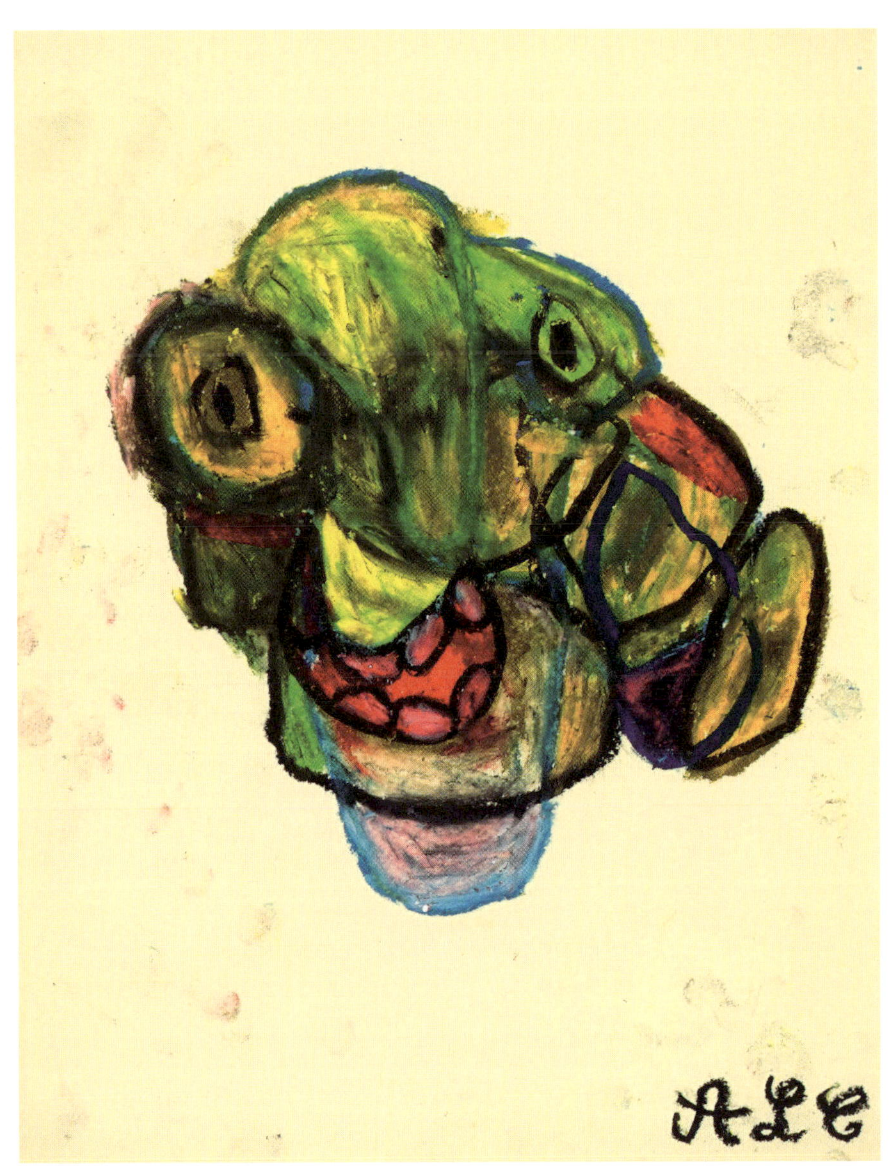
ALC

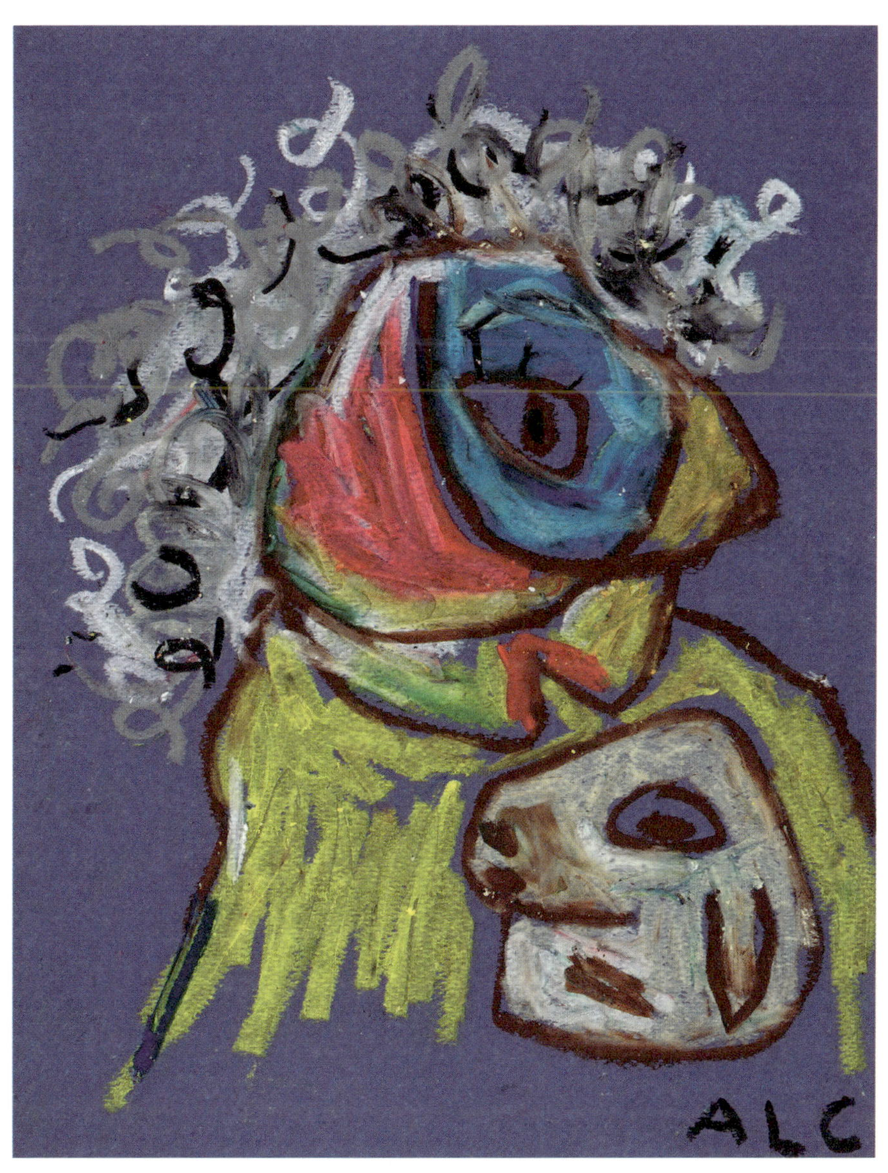
ALC

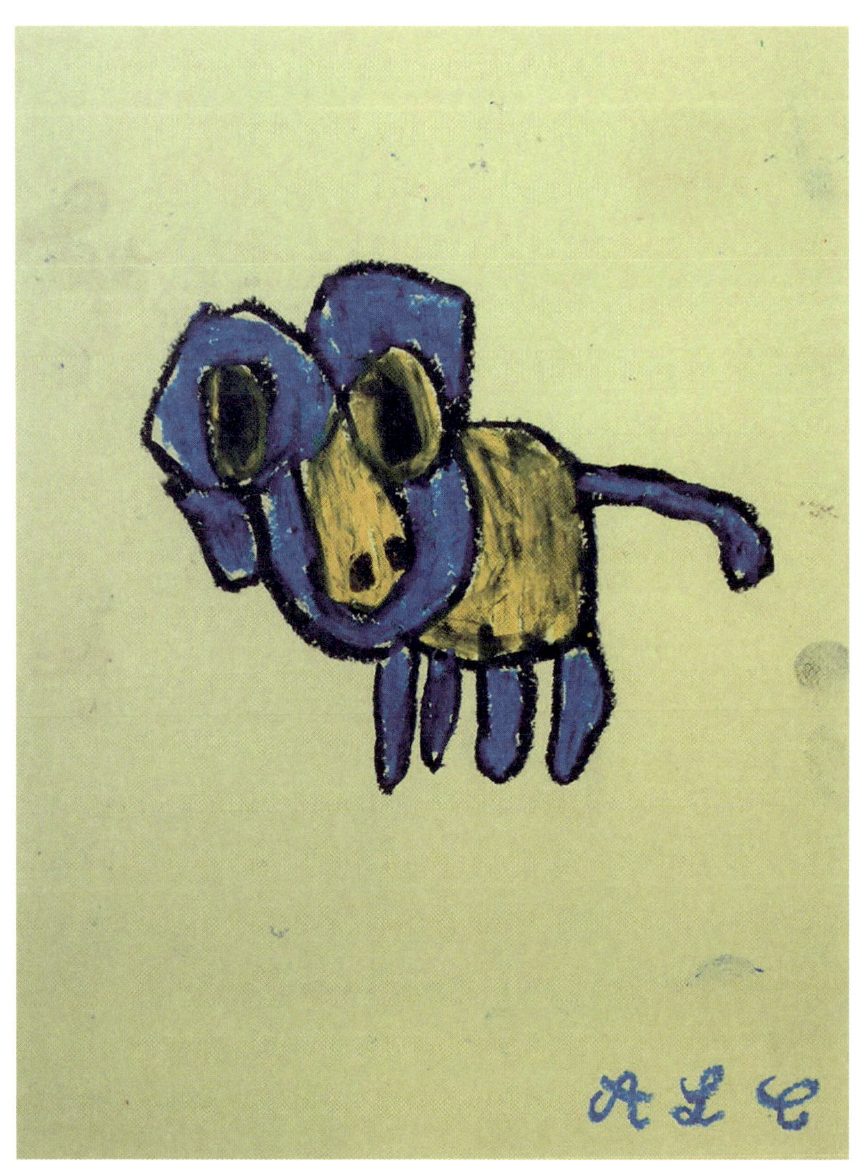
A L C

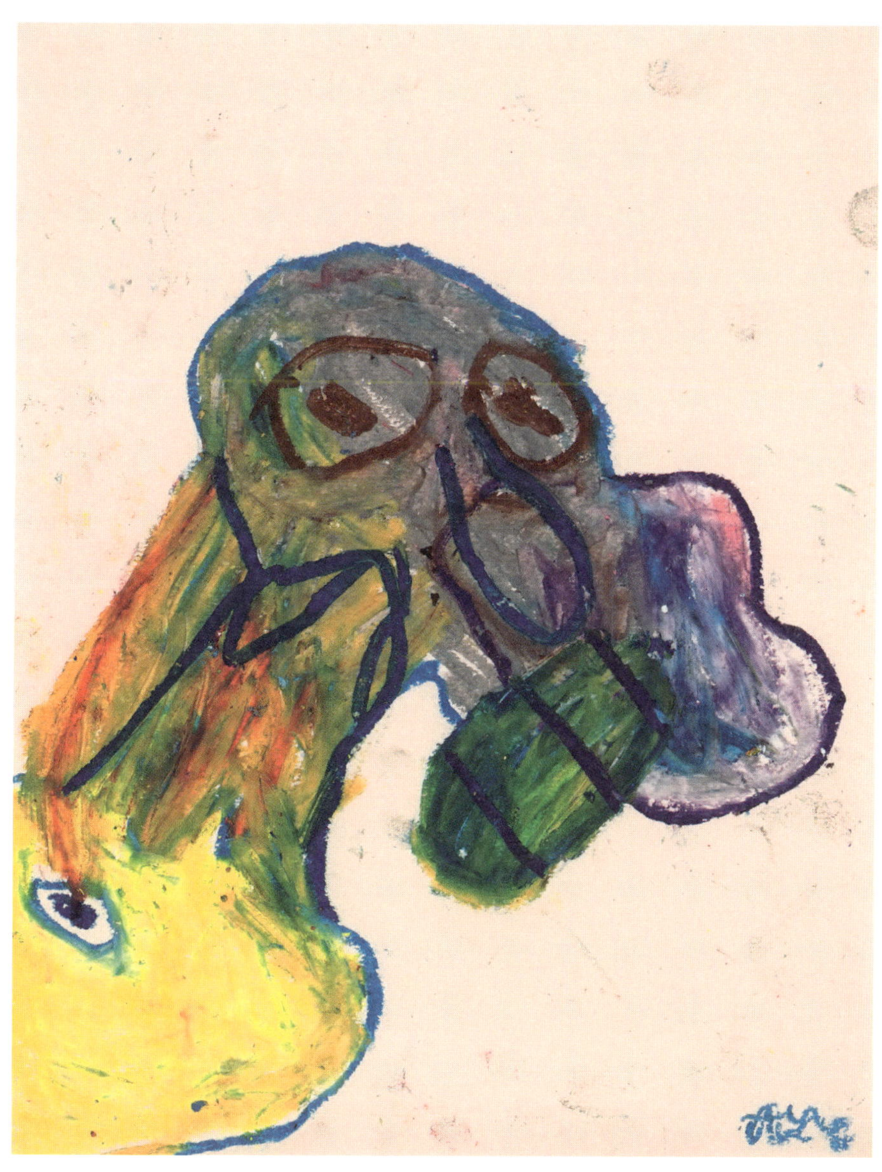

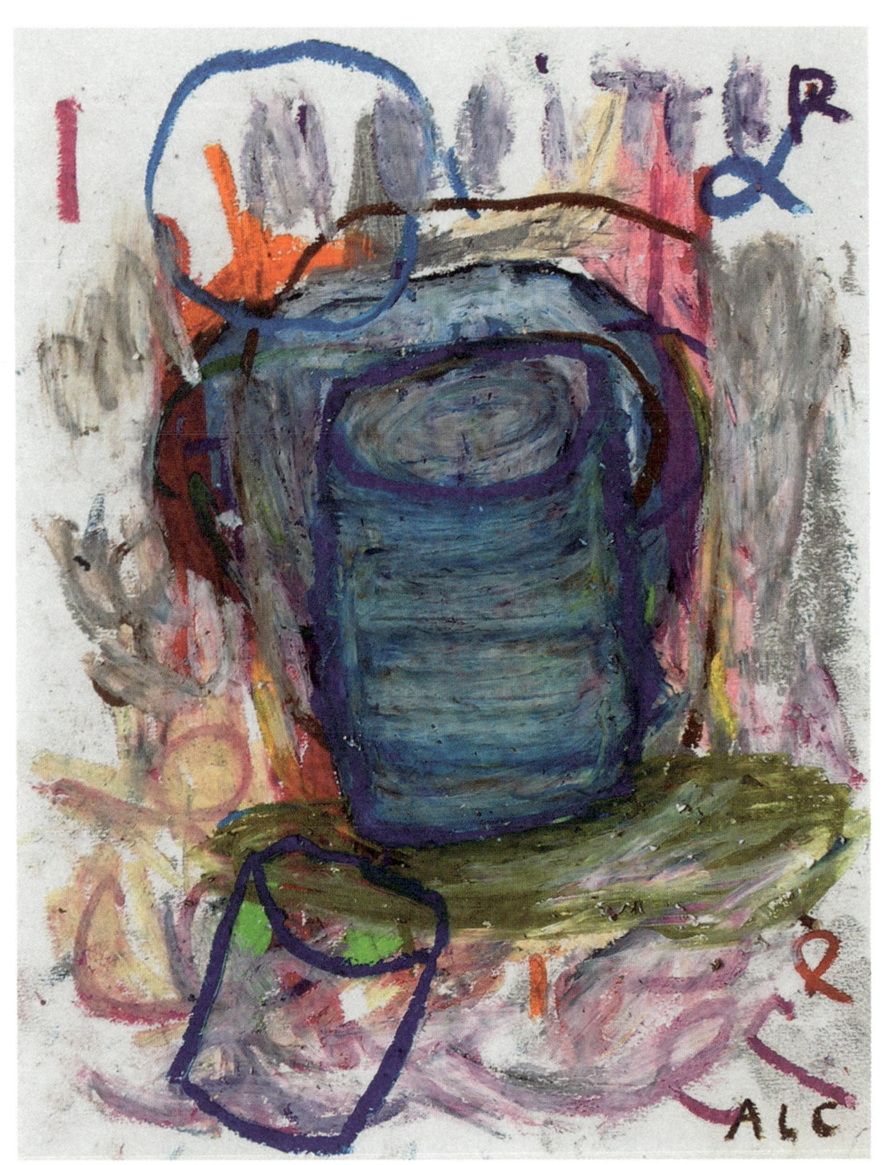
ALC

Text & Index

All or Nothing
Simon Maurer

Is Anne-Lise delicate, sensitive and vulnerable or rather more raw, harsh and powerful? It's hard to say. Maybe those qualities are not antagonistic. Her work is about the power of delicacy. And about the delicacy of power. And about the vulnerability of rawness. And about the rawness of vulnerability. And about the harshness of sensitivity. And about the sensitivity of harshness. Life is complicated and simple. Simplicity is complex. And complexity simple. The body obeys the mind. And the mind the body. And they don't obey each other. The body does what it wants. And the mind does, too. The body hates the mind. The mind hates the body. They fight with each other. The body wants one thing, the mind another. Why are they both in one and the same person? Why can't people just use their minds – without bodies? Why can't they have physical sensations – without their minds? They want to eliminate the mind. Kill it. Squeeze it out. They want to be all body. But the mind refuses to be battered to death. The minute you think it's dead, it acts up again. Comes to life again. Mind alone doesn't work either. The mind has to go to the loo. To pee and poo. Mind and body: they both want to escape their host. People are condemned to living with their bodies. And their minds. They can adapt both – but only sort of. Living means learning, coping with the body and the mind. Living means fighting self-hate. Learning to love oneself. The strengths and the weaknesses. Learning to accept what can't be changed, both physically and mentally. Living means learning to make fighting with yourself more tolerable. Being nicer to yourself. Less harsh.

What happens when a hand, an arm refuses to obey the mind? Which side yields? For Anne-Lise, neither and both, back and forth. A long time ago she learned to empty her mind before setting down to work: primal gestures. She has learned to appreciate what the arm, the hand can do – if you give them the chance. She has learned to trust her body. "We are all monkeys," she says. Her lines are harsh, clumsy, vehement, tender. Harsh tenderness, tender harshness. Opposites holding hands again. The lines seek autonomy. They want to break out. Out of the motifs. Out of art. They want to shatter the format. They do not want to please. But they have to yield to the composition. The battle between opposition and conformity takes place in the format of art. And there has to be a result. A physical one. A piece of paper, a canvas. If there were nothing there, the battle would be lost. Art would have ruined itself. So much for life. You have to abide by its format. If you get washed out, you have to watch from the sidelines, try to get back in. If it takes too long, you're done for. The battle of art is the battle to keep making art. Stopping and starting up again. It's a beautiful, vehement, tender battle. A battle with and against yourself.

Anne-Lise – I was a little in love with you, just briefly. We were so close. Almost the same size. Both tall, both thin. Almost anorexic. We were a woman who would also like to be a man, and we were a man who would also like to be a woman. Almost loved one another. But it didn't work. There was something heavy in between. Provence was too far away. I've never been there. I dreamt of the scents, the herbs, the animals, the bread, the wine. I dreamt of the landscapes, the sunsets, the hotels, the hideaways. But it didn't work. There was something in between. Maybe the gender. Maybe we were too similar, but different. Instead you gave me an exhibition. I loved it: the tall, white gallery filled with colourful paintings. Very big ones and very small ones. Very beautiful and very terrible. Horror and bonne vie as neighbours. Both exposed on white walls. Sometimes the sunlight threw crosses – window mullions – wandering across the paintings. Crosses on the paintings at night too, from the spotlights. The crosses didn't move at night. Gone again in the daytime. La bonne vie. The refugees.

During the exhibition, I was standing in front of the art school waiting for the tram. A man from Africa approached me. He wanted to know when the train was leaving for Munich - right here at the tram stop. I accompanied him to the main station. He was from Guinea. On the way, after a prolonged silence, I told him that a forward from Guinea had shot a lot of goals for my football club. That we called him the "Little Prince" and revered him. And that I once met him with his father in front of the town hall and told his father how proud we were of his son. And how that conjured a big smile on the faces of father and son. The refugee's face relaxed, softened a little. At the main station, I was in a quandary. Should I get him a ticket for a slow connection or a fast one? I tried to explain. At first I thought that if he took a slow connection, there would be less chance of being checked by border guards. Then I realized he'd never travelled by train before and he would have to change four times. So I got a ticket for the express train after all. Walked all the way to the back of the concourse with him, where there weren't as many officials. Explained to him what to do at the border. He said God would decide whether he makes it or not. We said goodbye - warmly. His name was Ernest. Afterwards I kept wondering whether I shouldn't have put him on the slow trains after all. It occurred to me that my decision could make or break his future. I wondered why I had helped him leave Switzerland in the first place. He wanted to leave badly. He had nothing - nothing at all. No bag, nothing. He was wearing a T-shirt and a light coat. That was it - just the clothes on his back.

Ernest. That was his name. The earnestness of the bonne vie. The gaieté. The joie de vivre. Was all that still possible? After everything we'd experienced, after everything that was happening right around us? That, too, is juxtaposed in Anne-Lise's work. That, too, is something she forces herself to bear: the proximity, the simultaneity. Of happiness and horror.

That, too, had to be. The authenticity. Being honest with oneself. And with art. The battle with art. The sincere, goal-oriented, single-minded, stubborn, persistent pursuit of a goal: and being able to look oneself in the eye afterwards. Thank you, Anne-Lise.

When we conducted an artist's conversation at Helmhaus, someone asked what you would do without art. I can't remember the exact wording of your reply. Only the gist of it. What would you be without art? It's a good thing it and you exist.

Translation by Catherine Schelbert

Index

40 *La beauté du paysage ne faiblit pas 1*, 2016
Pastel on paper
40 x 30 cm

41 *La beauté du paysage ne faiblit pas 2*, 2016
Pastel on paper
40 x 30 cm

42 *La beauté du paysage ne faiblit pas 3*, 2016
Pastel on paper
40 x 30 cm

43 *La beauté du paysage ne faiblit pas 4*, 2016
Pastel on paper
40 x 30 cm

44-45 *Samedi matin 1-3*, 2016
Pastel on paper, triptych
each 36 x 25 cm

46 *HOU*, 2016
Pastel on paper
31 x 24 cm

47 *Jour Jour*, 2016
Pastel on paper
31 x 24 cm

48 *Les migrants ont peur*, 2016
Pastel on paper
31 x 24 cm

49 *Me Crying*, 2016
Pastel on paper
36 x 25 cm

50 *Autoportrait aux bras levés*, 2016
Pastel on paper
31 x 24 cm

51 *Me Enjoying*, 2016
Pastel on paper
36 x 25 cm

52 *Me Sun*, 2016
Pastel on paper
31 x 24 cm

53 *Me Very Sad*, 2016
Pastel on paper
31 x 24 cm

54 *Me Wondering*, 2016
Pastel on paper
36 x 25 cm

55 *Moi sauvée par l'Art*, 2016
Pastel on paper
39 x 30 cm

56 *My Bedroom 1*, 2016
Pastel on paper
31 x 24 cm

57 *My Bedroom*, 2016
Pastel on paper
31 x 24 cm

58 *Self Portrait (Orange)*, 2016
Pastel on paper
31 x 24 cm

59 *Self Portrait in Blue*, 2016
Pastel on paper
23 x 16 cm

60 *Talisman (I Phone)*, 2016
Pastel on paper
23 x 16 cm

61 *L'élan vital*, 2016
Pastel on paper
31 x 24 cm

62 *Untitled (with Blue Lines)*, 2016
Pastel on paper
23 x 16 cm

63 *Yellow Interior*, 2016
Pastel on paper
19.5 x 14.5 cm

64 *Kissing*, 2016
Pastel on paper
32 x 24 cm

65 *Untitled*, 2016
Pastel on paper
32 x 24 cm

66 *Self Portrait*, 2016
Pastel on paper
32 x 24 cm

67 *Catherine et Joy*, 2016
Pastel on paper
32 x 24 cm

68 *Le chien jaune et bleu*, 2016
Pastel on paper
32 x 24 cm

69 *Untitled*, 2016
Pastel on paper
32 x 24 cm

70 *Le verre*, 2016
Pastel on paper
32 x 24 cm

Alles oder nichts
Simon Maurer

Es ist schwer zu sagen, was ausgeprägter ist an Anne-Lise: das Feine, Empfindsame, Verletzliche oder das Rohe, Harte, Kräftige. Vielleicht sind das ja keine antagonistischen Qualitäten. Sondern es geht hier um die Kraft des Feinen. Und um die Feinheit des Kräftigen. Um die Verletzlichkeit des Rohen. Und um das Rohe des Verletzlichen. Um die Härte der Empfindsamkeit. Und um die Empfindsamkeit des Harten. Das Leben ist kompliziert und einfach. Das Einfache ist kompliziert. Und das Komplizierte einfach. Der Körper gehorcht dem Denken. Und das Denken dem Körper. Und beide gehorchen einander nicht. Der Körper macht, was er will. Und das Denken auch. Der Körper hasst das Denken. Das Denken hasst den Körper. Beide kämpfen miteinander. Der Körper will das eine, das Denken das andere. Warum stecken beide in der gleichen Person? Warum kann die Person nicht nur denken – ohne Körper? Warum kann sie nicht nur körperliche Empfindungen haben – ohne zu denken? Die Person möchte das Denken ausschalten. Sie möchte es töten. Sie möchte es aus sich herauspressen. Sie möchte nur noch Körper sein. Aber das Denken lässt sich nicht totschlagen. Kaum meint man, es ist tot, regt es sich erneut. Und beginnt wieder zu leben. Das reine Denken geht aber auch nicht. Das Denken muss aufs Klo. Es macht Pipi und Kaka. Beide, das Denken und der Körper, möchten fliehen aus der Person. Aber die Person ist verdammt dazu, mit ihrem Körper zu leben. Und mit ihrem Denken. Sie kann beides anpassen – aber nur bedingt. Leben heisst lernen, mit seinem Körper und mit seinem Denken umzugehen. Leben heisst, den Hass gegen sich selber zu bekämpfen. Sich lieben lernen... Die eigenen Stärken. Und die Schwächen. Das, was man an sich nicht verändern kann, an seinem Körper und an seinem Denken, akzeptieren zu lernen. Leben heisst lernen, den Kampf mit sich selber erträglicher zu führen. Netter zu sich zu sein. Weniger hart.

Wenn die Hand, der Arm nicht will, was der Kopf will? Wer gehorcht wem? Bei Anne-Lise geht es hin und her. Sie hat lange gelernt, den Kopf auszuleeren, bevor sie arbeitet: 'primal gestures'. Sie hat zu schätzen gelernt, was der Arm, die Hand macht – wenn man sie denn lässt. Sie hat gelernt, dem Körper zu vertrauen. 'We are all monkeys', sagt sie. Ihr Strich ist hart, ist ungelenk, ist heftig, ist zärtlich. Wieder: die harte Zärtlichkeit, das zärtlich Harte. Die Striche suchen die Selbständigkeit. Sie wollen ausbrechen. Aus den Motiven. Aus der Kunst. Sie wollen das Format sprengen. Sie wollen nicht gefallen. Aber sie müssen der Komposition gehorchen. Der Kampf zwischen Opposition und Anpassung findet auf dem Format der Kunst statt. Letztlich muss ein Resultat da sein. Etwas Physisches. Ein Blatt Papier, eine Leinwand. Wenn nichts da wäre, wäre der Kampf verloren. Dann hätte sich Kunst kaputtgemacht. Dann wäre das Leben dahin. Es geht darum, in diesem Format zu bleiben. Wer rausfliegt, muss zusehen, darauf zurückzukommen. Wer länger draussen bleibt, ist fertig, kaputt. Der Kampf der Kunst ist der Kampf, weiter Kunst zu machen. Aufzuhören und wieder anzufangen. Es ist ein brutaler, ein heftiger, ein zärtlicher Kampf. Ein Kampf mit und gegen sich selbst.

Anne-Lise – ich war ganz kurz ein wenig verliebt in Dich. Wir waren uns so nah. Fast gleich gross. Beide gross, beide dünn. Fast magersüchtig. Wir waren eine Frau, die auch gern ein Mann wäre. Und wir waren ein Mann, der auch gern eine Frau wäre. Wir liebten uns fast. Aber es ging nicht. Irgendwas war schwer dazwischen. Die Provence war zu weit weg. Ich war noch nie da. Ich träumte von den Düften, den Kräutern, den Tieren, den Broten, dem Wein. Ich träumte von den Landschaften, den Sonnenuntergängen, den Hotels, den Hide-aways. Aber es ging nicht. Etwas war dazwischen. Vielleicht die Geschlechter. Vielleicht waren wir uns zu ähnlich, aber anders. Du hast mir stattdessen eine Ausstellung geschenkt. Ich liebte sie: diesen weissen, hohen Saal mit diesen farbigen Bildern. Ganz grossen und ganz kleinen. Ganz schönen und ganz schrecklichen. Terror und 'bonne vie' als Nachbarn. Beide entblösst auf weissen Wänden. Manchmal kam die Sonne und liess mit den Schatten der Fensterkreuze Kreuze über die Bilder wandern. Nachts gingen draussen die Scheinwerfer an und warfen erneut Kreuze über die Bilder. Nachts standen die Kreuze still. Am Tag waren sie wieder weg. La bonne vie. Die Flüchtlinge.

Während der Ausstellung wartete ich an der Tramhaltestelle vor der Kunsthochschule. Ein Mann aus Afrika kam auf mich zu. Er fragte mich, wann hier ein Zug nach München fährt. Er meinte: hier, an der Tramhaltestelle... Ich brachte ihn zum Hauptbahnhof. Er kam aus Guinea. Auf der Fahrt, nach längerer Stille, erzählte ich ihm, dass einmal ein kleiner Stürmer aus Guinea viele Tore für meinen Fussballclub geschossen hat. Dass wir ihn 'Kleiner Prinz' nannten. Dass wir ihn verehrten - und ich ihn einmal vor dem Stadthaus mit seinem Vater antraf und dem Vater sagte, wie stolz wir auf seinen Sohn seien. Und wie dieser Satz ein breites Lächeln auf die Gesichter von Vater und Sohn zauberte. Das Gesicht des Geflüchteten entspannte sich ein wenig. Im Hauptbahnhof überlegte ich lange und erklärte ihm meine Zweifel, ob er ein Ticket für eine langsame oder eine schnelle Verbindung nehmen sollte. Erst dachte ich: 'Langsam, da sind die Chancen wesentlich grösser, dass er nicht in eine Grenzkontrolle kommt.' Dann merkte ich, dass es für ihn ganz neu war, Züge zu benutzen, und dass er viermal umsteigen müsste. Da gab ich ihm ein Ticket für den schnellen Zug. Ging mit ihm bis ans Ende der Bahnhofshalle, weil er da weniger kontrolliert würde. Besprach mit ihm, was er am Grenzübergang tun sollte. Er sagte, Gott werde entscheiden, ob er es schafft oder nicht. Wir verabschiedeten uns herzlich. Er hiess Ernest. Ich dachte nachher immer wieder darüber nach, ob ich ihn nicht doch besser auf die langsamen Züge gebracht hätte. Ich dachte, dass ich mit diesem Entscheid vielleicht über ein Lebensschicksal entschieden hatte. Ich fragte mich, ob er es geschafft hat, nach Deutschland zu kommen. Ich fragte mich, warum ich ihm geholfen hatte, die Schweiz zu verlassen. Er wollte es unbedingt. Er hatte absolut nichts dabei. Keine Tasche, nichts. Er trug ein T-Shirt und einen leichten Mantel darüber. Sonst hatte er: nichts.

Ernest. Er hiess so. Der Ernst der 'bonne vie'. 'La gaieté'. Die 'joie de vivre'. War das alles noch möglich? Nach allem, was wir erlebt haben, nach allem, was sich in unserer unmittelbaren Nähe abspielte? Auch das kommt zusammen bei Anne-Lise. Auch das zwingt sie, sich auszuhalten: diese Nähe, diese Gleichzeitigkeit. Von Glück und Horror.

Es musste so sein. Diese Authentizität. Diese Ehrlichkeit zu sich selbst. Und zur Kunst. Dieser Kampf mit der Kunst. Diese 'sincérité', diese Orientierung, dieses Ziel, diese Beharrlichkeit, diese Konsequenz auf dieses Ziel hin: sich selbst danach in die Augen sehen zu können. Danke, Anne-Lise.

Bei dem Künstlergespräch, das wir im Helmhaus führten, fragte jemand, was Du tun würdest ohne die Kunst. Ich weiss nicht mehr genau, was Du geantwortet hast. Nur der Sinn ist mir noch gegenwärtig. Was wärst Du ohne Kunst? Gut, dass es sie und Dich gibt.

Anne-Lise Coste

Oil Paintings and Pastel Drawings

Nieves